AMIGURUMI ADVENTURES

FEATURING 21 PLAYFUL CROCHET DESIGNS

CLARE COOPER

Tuva Publishing
www.tuvapublishing.com

Address Merkez Mah. Cavusbasi Cad. No71
Cekmekoy - Istanbul 34782 / Turkey
Tel +9 0216 642 62 62

Amigurumi Adventures

First Print October 2023

All Global Copyrights Belong To
Tuva Tekstil ve Yayıncılık Ltd.

Content Crochet

Editor in Chief Ayhan DEMİRPEHLİVAN
Project Editor Kader DEMİRPEHLİVAN
Designers Clare COOPER
Technical Editor Leyla ARAS
Graphic Designers Ömer ALP, Abdullah BAYRAKÇI,
Tarık TOKGÖZ, Yunus GÜLDOĞAN
Photography Tuva Publishing
Crochet Tech Editor Wendi CUSINS

ISBN 978-605-7834-79-9

 TuvaYayincilik    TuvaPublishing

 TuvaYayincilik   TuvaPublishing

INTRODUCTION

Welcome to my amigurumi adventures! I'm so excited you're here. We're going to meet a trio of sweet little cactus dolls, a busy bee, a shy grapefruit girl, friends on safari, and young Amity, dressed ready for any adventure. Our travels will take us across the globe to meet dolls in traditional dress, and then back again to discover some lovable characters, perfect for gifting to someone special.

The concept for my curious flat-headed dolls was inspired by the traditional, homemade rag doll. These simple cloth figures, made by stitching together panels of scrap fabric, date back as far as early Roman times and have appeared in numerous cultures around the world. I love the idea that a cherished child's toy can be created from leftover material that may otherwise be thrown away. But what really appealed to me was the simplicity of this method of doll making and the endearing nature of hand embroidered features.

Like the rag doll, the heads of my crocheted dolls are worked as two flat sections (front and back). This differs from a standard amigurumi style doll made with a spherical head and gives my dolls a cute appearance. I've found there are a few advantages to working this way, the main one being the preservation of a cute, oversized head without the weight of a larger sphere. The dolls' hair can also be playfully styled without the need to construct a wig or to attach a full head of individual strands, and you have a flat surface on which to embroider those sweet little faces.

On that note, I should confess I have somewhat of a love-hate relationship with hand embroidery. I love the charming aesthetic of simple hand sewn features and wanted to invoke that innocent rag doll style. The challenge however lies in embroidering symmetrical features on an uneven crochet fabric, where small variations in stitch placement quickly alter the overall look of the doll. If you too find this task a little daunting, you are not alone. I hope the tools and embroidery method I've described in this book will help you feel confident to practice and experiment until you achieve the look you're after.

As for the bodies of the dolls, they are made in a more traditional amigurumi style, and (you may be pleased to discover) require no sewing. The bodies were sized with my children's small hands in mind. They can be gripped comfortably around the middle, and clutched tight to the chest as a night time companion.

One of the most enjoyable aspects of designing these dolls has been in the detail; playing with colors, fussing over a hair curl or accessory, trialing stitch combinations to achieve a particular texture or finish. I feel like there's always so much to learn and so much opportunity for creativity.

With that said, it's over to you now! I hope these little ones inspire you to pick up your crochet hook and bring them to life.

Love Clare x

PROJECT GALLERY

RUBY THE GRAPEFRUIT GIRL
P.30

AMITY - THE ADVENTURER
P. 36

SCARLETT
P. 62

MARIGOLD
P. 68

FREYA
P. 74

CACTUS GIRLS
P.80

ANIMALS
P.96

MYRTLE THE BEE
P. 114

WORLD DOLLS
P.120

CONTENTS

PROJECTS

Materials & Tools

Crochet & Amigurumi Basics

TOOLS AND MATERIALS

YARN

All the designs in this book were made using **HELLO Cotton Yarn**. I love working with cotton for my amigurumi, especially one with a matte (unmercerised) finish. In addition to being a natural plant fiber, cotton yarn produces lovely stitch definition and holds its shape well, with little stretch. You may, of course, substitute with a yarn of your choice; cotton blends are also very popular.

CROCHET HOOKS

There are a variety of crochet hooks available on the market and which to choose depends very much on personal preference. Stainless steel and aluminum hooks are well suited to working with cotton yarns, and I prefer using ones with an ergonomic rubber grip. All the dolls in this book were made using my trusty Clover Amour **2.5 mm hook**. For some elements, I've used a **2 mm or 3 mm hook**, which is noted where applicable.

Depending on the weight of yarn you have selected and your natural "gauge" (tension), adjust your hook size to ensure you are creating a dense fabric through which stuffing will not show. As a general guide, the hook should be at least half a millimeter smaller than suggested by the yarn manufacturer. The size of your finished doll may vary from the design but the overall proportions will be retained.

STUFFING

Most often I use a polyester (synthetic) **fiberfill** for stuffing my amigurumi. It is soft, lightweight and readily available from craft stores. Fiberfill is also hypoallergenic and washes easily, so is perfectly suited to making toys.

There are more environmentally-friendly options available, such as corn and eucalyptus fibers. Many of their attributes are similar to that of synthetic fiberfill, particularly with regard to softness and texture. But natural fibers do behave slightly differently; they are heavier and tend to compact a little more over time.

ACCESSORIES

Stitch Markers

As amigurumi is worked in a continuous spiral, using a stitch marker to identify the first (or last) stitch of the round is very helpful. It needn't be fancy; a scrap of yarn or hair pin work fine. I like to use locking stitch markers, which are great if you are putting your project aside to pick up again later.

Needles

For all the patterns in this book you will need two types of needles:

Yarn (Tapestry) Needle with a blunt tip and large eye (suitable for threading yarn) for weaving in loose ends and sewing different pieces of crochet together. The blunt tip allows the needle to pass under individual fibers of yarn without splitting or snagging. I prefer steel needles over plastic as they are easier to work between tight stitches.

Embroidery Needle with a sharp tip for embroidering the face and other details. Unlike a yarn needle, an embroidering needle allows you to more easily work into the crochet fabric by splitting the yarn strands (rather than working between stitches). By doing so, the embroidered stitches are placed more securely and with greater precision.

Embroidery Floss

The faces of my dolls are embroidered using black, six-stranded cotton embroidery floss. You may use the full thickness or remove one or two strands for slightly finer features, as I like to do.

Dress-making Pins

For the dolls in this book, I use dress-making pins mainly for securing the hair or hood to the head before sewing. You may also use pins as a guide for the face embroidery, to mark the positions of the eyes and mouth. Select ones with a rounded plastic or glass head to avoid losing them inside your work.

Scissors

Small, lightweight scissors with a sharp point are perfect for amigurumi.

Other Bits and Pieces

Useful items to have on hand include a pom-pom maker, small buttons or snap fasteners and make-up blush (to give your dolls an extra rosy-cheeked finish). A small wooden dowel is perfect for prodding stuffing into tight spaces (chopsticks work well too). I also like to have a cup of tea (or beverage of choice) within arms reach!

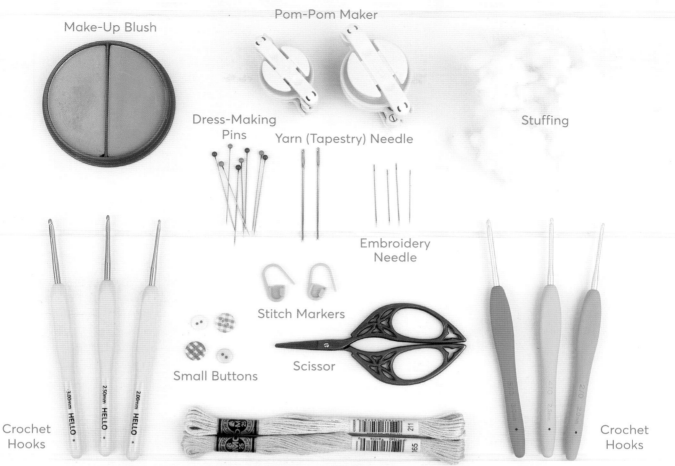

Make-Up Blush

Pom-Pom Maker

Dress-Making Pins

Yarn (Tapestry) Needle

Stuffing

Embroidery Needle

Stitch Markers

Small Buttons

Scissor

Crochet Hooks

Crochet Hooks

Embroidery Floss

HELLO Cotton Yarn

CROCHET BASICS

HOLDING THE HOOK AND YARN

If you are just starting out with crochet, holding the hook and yarn can feel a little awkward. With practice this will quickly change! It is usual to hold the hook with your dominant hand, and the yarn with the other, using either a **pencil** or **knife** grip. Adopt a method that feels most comfortable for you, there is no right or wrong.

There are many more ways that crocheters hold the yarn with their free hand, but essentially, you need to control the yarn so the stitches are worked with consistent tension. Personally, I hold the yarn by wrapping it around my pinky finger to secure, and then lay it over the top of my index finger to create a **working space** for wrapping the yarn with my crochet hook.

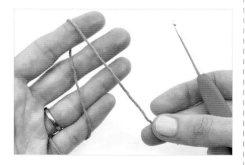

SLIP KNOT

The first loop on your hook is a slip knot, and does not count as a stitch (nor will it be mentioned in the pattern, it is assumed). There are various ways to make a slip knot, so feel free to find a method that works best for you.

Form a loop with the yarn, keeping the tail end of the yarn behind the working yarn (i.e. the yarn connected to the ball). Hold the loop in place using your fingers.

Pass your hook through the loop (from front to back) and catch the working yarn with the hook.

Draw the yarn back through the loop.

Keeping the loop of yarn on the hook, release the starting loop and pull the tail end to tighten the knot.

Pull the working yarn to slide the knot towards the hook.

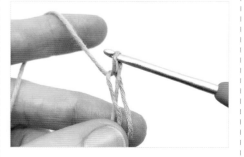

WRAPPING THE YARN

With a slip knot on your hook, you are ready to start crocheting! Holding the hook in front of the working space, use your hook to catch the working yarn from below, wrapping the yarn **over** the hook from back to front. This action is referred to as a **"yarn over" (YO)** and forms an essential part of all crochet stitches.

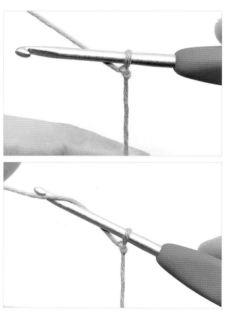

CHAIN STITCH (CH)

After catching the yarn, draw it through the loop on your hook. You have just completed your first chain stitch! Repeat this action of yarning over and drawing the yarn through the loop on your hook to create additional chains, holding the yarn tail firmly to prevent the loop spinning on your hook. The front of your chain will look like a series of nested letter "V"s, while the back of the chain has a line of small ridges (referred to as **back bumps**).

If working in rows, the chain stitches will form the initial row, referred to as the **foundation chain** or **starting chain**. I use my thumb and middle finger to hold the tail of the slip knot and my index finger to guide the yarn. It is helpful to change your grip on the crocheted chains as you go along, keeping your fingers close to the hook to maintain even stitch tension.

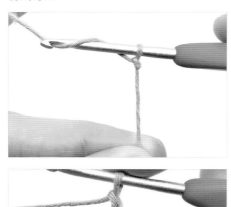

STITCH ANATOMY

With the exception of chain stitches, all crochet stitches need to be worked into existing stitches. Understanding the anatomy of the stitch is helpful for knowing where to insert your hook. Each basic stitch comprises two **top loops**, which look like a horizontal letter "V" when viewed from above. These are identified as the **front loop** (the loop closest to you when you hold your work) and the **back loop** (the loop furthest away).

Back Loop   Both Loops   Front Loop

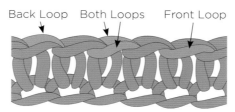

A vertical **post** below these top loops forms the body of the stitch. The height of the post varies depending on the type of stitch worked; the post is very short for a single crochet and gradually increases in height for double crochet, treble crochet, etc.

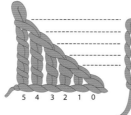

5 Double Treble Crochet
4 Treble Crochet
3 Double Crochet
2 Half-Double Crochet
1 Single Crochet
0 Slip Stitch

5 4 3 2 1 0

Unless otherwise specified in the pattern, **the hook is inserted under both top loops of the next stitch** in the round or row below. (We'll talk more about working into a foundation chain in *"Working in to Different Loops"* on pages 15 and 16.

COUNTING STITCHES

Learning how to count stitches is important for any crochet project. Among other things, an accurate stitch count means you're on track with following the pattern. The easiest way to do this is to look for the "V"s along the top of each stitch (the **working loop** on your hook does not count as a stitch). Whether you count your stitches as you work them, or do a quick check at the end of each round, ensure your count equals the number of stitches specified in the pattern.

Front of Chain
6 chain stitches

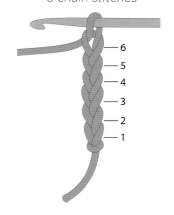

6
5
4
3
2
1

BASIC STITCH GUIDE

SLIP STITCH (SL ST)

The slip stitch is the smallest of the basic stitches, and allows you to move along a piece of crochet work without adding any height or increasing the size of the work. In this way, it is great for strengthening the edge of a crochet piece. The slip stitch is also used to join the ends of a foundation chain to form a ring and to close off a round.

Starting with a loop on your hook, insert hook in stitch (or space) specified. Yarn over and draw yarn through both the stitch **and** the loop on your hook.

Note: the following descriptions use **US crochet terminology.** *Refer to the table included in* **Abbreviations** *(page 27) for the equivalent UK terms.*

SINGLE CROCHET (SC)

This humble little stitch is the basis for all crocheted amigurumi. It produces a tight fabric to maintain the shape of the toy and contain the stuffing.

Starting with a loop on your hook, insert hook in stitch (or space) specified. Yarn over and pull yarn through the stitch (2 loops on hook). Yarn over again and draw yarn through both loops on hook.

Tip: The instruction to "yarn over and pull yarn through the stitch" is also described as "pulling up a loop" (i.e., you are creating an extra loop on your hook).

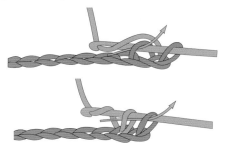

The following stitches gradually increase in height, from the half double crochet up to the treble crochet. I use these stitches throughout the hair and clothing of my dolls.

HALF-DOUBLE CROCHET (HDC)

Starting with a loop on your hook, yarn over before inserting hook in stitch (or space) specified. Yarn over and pull yarn through the stitch (3 loops on hook). Yarn over and draw yarn through all 3 loops on hook.

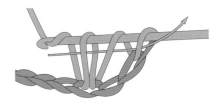

DOUBLE CROCHET (DC)

Starting with a loop on your hook, yarn over before inserting hook in stitch (or space) specified. Yarn over and pull yarn through the stitch (3 loops on hook). Yarn over and draw yarn through first 2 loops (2 loops remain on hook). Yarn over and draw yarn through remaining 2 loops on hook.

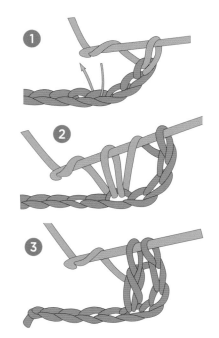

TREBLE CROCHET (TR)

Starting with a loop on your hook, yarn over twice before inserting hook in stitch (or space) specified. Yarn over and pull yarn though the stitch (4 loops on hook). Yarn over and draw yarn through first 2 loops (3 loops remain on hook). Yarn over and draw yarn through first 2 loops again (2 loops remain on hook). Yarn over and draw yarn through remaining 2 loops on hook.

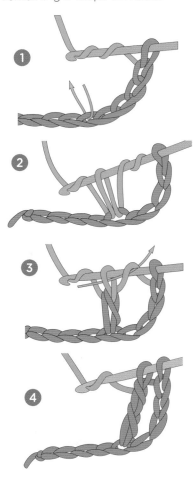

INCREASING AND DECREASING

Increase and decrease stitches are used to shape a crochet piece. Work two (or more) stitches into the same stitch to **increase** the stitch count of the round, making the work wider. Work two (or more) stitches together to **decrease** the number of stitches, making the work narrower.

Standard Single Crochet Increase (inc)

Insert hook into stitch and complete first single crochet. Insert hook into the **same stitch** and complete second single crochet.

Standard Single Crochet Decrease (dec)

Insert hook into first stitch, yarn over and pull yarn through stitch (2 loops on hook). Insert hook into second stitch and pull yarn though stitch (3 loops on hook). Yarn over and draw through all 3 loops on hook.

Standard Half-Double Crochet Decrease (hdc-dec)

Yarn over, insert hook into first stitch, yarn over and pull yarn through the stitch (3 loops on hook). Insert hook into second stitch, yarn over and pull yarn through the stitch (4 loops on hook). Yarn over and draw through all 4 loops on hook.

Standard Double Crochet Decrease (dc-dec)

Yarn over, insert hook into first stitch, yarn over and pull yarn through stitch (3 loops on hook). Yarn over and draw yarn through first 2 loops (2 loops remain on hook). Yarn over, insert hook into second stitch, yarn over and pull yarn through stitch (4 loops on hook). Yarn over and draw through first 2 loops (3 loops remain on hook). Yarn over and draw through all 3 loops on hook.

Tip: Notice that decrease stitches are made by working unfinished stitches (i.e., stitches worked until just before the last "yarn over and pull through remaining loops on hook") that are then drawn together.

Standard Treble Crochet Decrease (tr-dec)

Yarn over twice, insert hook into first stitch, yarn over and pull yarn through stitch (4 loops on hook). Yarn over and draw through first 2 loops (3 loops remain on hook), yarn over and draw through first 2 loops again (2 loops remain on hook). Yarn over twice and insert hook into second stitch, yarn over and pull yarn through stitch (5 loops on hook). Yarn over and draw yarn through first 2 loops on hook (4 loops remain on hook), yarn over and draw through first 2 loops again (3 loops remain on hook). Yarn over and draw through all 3 loops on hook.

CROCHET TECHNIQUES

Broadly speaking, there are two ways in which to work your crochet stitches; either in rounds or rows. Amigurumi is typically worked in continuous rounds as it produces a neat, seamless finish. All of the heads and bodies of my dolls are worked in this way.

WORKING IN ROUNDS

Rounds are used for creating circular pieces, which may be either flat or 3-dimensional. At the end of each round of stitches, continue on in one of two ways:

- Joined (closed) rounds are finished by working a slip stitch into the first stitch of the round. The next round starts with one or more initial chain stitches to raise the hook to the height of the stitches to be worked.

- Continuous (spiral) rounds are not closed with a slip stitch. To start the next round, crochet directly into the first stitch of the previous round. *For all the patterns in this book, work in continuous rounds unless otherwise specified.*

Using Stitch Markers

When working in continuous rounds, it is important to keep track of where one round ends and the next one begins. Using a stitch marker is the most common way to do this. I like to work the first few stitches of a round, and then mark the first stitch by sliding the stitch marker under the top loops of the stitch. At the completion of the round, the last stitch is worked in the stitch before the marked stitch.

Using a **running stitch marker** can be helpful for tracking the start of successive rounds and avoids having to move or replace your marker after each round. Before starting a new round, lay a length of yarn in a contrasting color across your work. Complete the instructed stitches, then at the end of the round, flip the length of yarn to the opposite side of the work. Continue in this way, flipping the yarn between the front and the back of the work as each round is completed. To remove, simply pull the length of yarn out of the work.

Twisting

The way that stitches stack on top of one another when working in the round means that the start of the round moves gradually to the right (or left, if you are left-handed) as rounds are completed (by approximately one stitch every three rounds). This is highlighted by the use of the running stitch marker (refer images above). I found this somewhat disconcerting when I first starting making amigurumi (particularly if working in a striped pattern, for which this phenomenon becomes more apparent) but rest assured, it is completely normal!

"Right" and "Wrong" Sides

Working in the round also means the resulting crochet fabric looks different on each side. As you crochet, the side facing you is referred to as the **right side** as the fronts of the stitches are visible. The backs of the stitches are referred to as the **wrong side**. All my patterns are designed with the right side facing out; the work appears neater and the horizontal back bars of the stitches are not visible.

Right Side

Wrong Side

WORKING IN ROWS

Rows are worked to create flat crochet pieces, typically (but not always) in a square or rectangular shape. After completing the instructed stitches, make the specified number of **turning chains** to bring the hook up to the height of the stitches to be worked, and **turn the work horizontally** to begin the next row.

Turning Chains

The number of turning chains will be depend on the height of the stitches to follow (and is specified in the pattern). As a general guide, one chain is used for single crochet stitches, two for half-double crochet, three for double crochet and four for treble crochet.

Personally, I find turning chains can be a source of confusion, particularly with respect to whether or not the turning chain "counts as a stitch". As the hair for many of my dolls is worked in rows, the inclusion (or exclusion) of the turning chain in the stitch count is important for achieving the correct shape in order to fit the face. So, here is a quick summary:

- As a general rule, a **turning chain of one does not count as a stitch**

- For turning chains of more than one, my patterns specify whether or not they count as a stitch.

This information is important as it determines where the first stitch of the row should be made and, in the following row, whether or not you work a stitch into the top of the turning chain from the previous row. This is summarized in the table below:

Turning Chain	Where to work the first stitch of the row	What to do in the following row
Does not count as a stitch	Into the **first stitch** (i.e. the **same stitch** that the turning chain is worked from)	Do not work into the top of the turning chain from the previous row
Counts as a stitch	Into the **next stitch** (i.e. the stitch after the one the turning chain is worked from)	Work into the top of the turning chain from previous row

WORKING INTO DIFFERENT LOOPS

As described in *Stitch Anatomy* *(page 11)*, all basic crochet stitches have two top loops under which your crochet hook is typically inserted to start a new stitch. Working into only one of either of these top loops, or another part of the stitch, changes the finish of the crochet fabric.

Back and Front Loops

Inserting the hook under the **back loop**, leaves the front loop as a horizontal bar on the right side of the work. Working successive stitches in this way creates a line of front loops that can be used for decorative purposes or to attach yarn. Similarly, working into the **front loop** leaves the back loop on the wrong side of the work.

Tip: The front loop is always the loop closest to you, irrespective of whether you are working on the right or wrong side of the work. Similarly, the back loop is always the loop furthest from you.

Half-Double Crochet "3rd Loops"

When working a half-double crochet stitch, the first "yarn over" that is made before inserting the hook into a stitch creates an extra loop, referred to as the "3rd loop". The loop can be identified by looking for the additional horizontal bar at the back of all half-double crochet stitches (try tilting the top loops towards you to get a better view). To work into the half-double crochet 3rd loop, insert your hook from the top down. This pushes the two top loops to the front of the work, creating a braid-like row of V shapes.

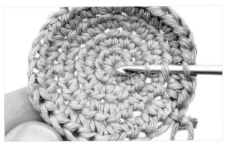

Foundation Chains

When working into the loops of a **foundation (starting) chain,** there are number of options. Inserting the hook into the **back bumps** will produce a neat edge with the two top loops visible and is the method I generally prefer. However, if the starting chain will not be noticeable (e.g., it will be sewn to another piece of crochet work), I find working into only the **back loop** (also referred to as the **"top" loop** of the chain) to be easier and quicker.

Tip: Ensuring the chains are worked with looser tension (or a slightly

larger hook) will make inserting your hook into the loops easier.

To work around both sides of a foundation chain, work stitches into each chain stitch until reaching the starting slip knot (you may choose whether you work into the back (top) loop, back bump, or both). From here, rotate the chain, and work back across the other side, using the remaining chain loops. Continue working in the round to create an oval shape (the proportions of which will be determined by the number of starting chains).

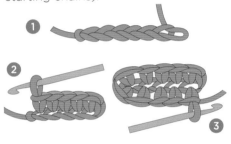

Row Ends

Sometimes you may be required to work into the sides of stitches, along the edge of your crochet piece, rather than into the top loops (applicable to a piece worked in rows). If you stretch your work a little, you will see small holes at the ends of the rows. Working stitches into these row ends is a great way of creating a border to neaten the edges of your work.

16

AMIGURUMI TECHNIQUES

There are a handful of techniques for improving the overall appearance of your amigurumi.

MAGIC RING (OR MAGIC CIRCLE)

The Magic Ring is one such technique, and is essential for any amigurumi project. It is used to begin crocheting in the round by working stitches over an adjustable loop. When the loop is pulled tight, the stitches are closed in a ring and the hole in the center is eliminated.

This technique can seem confusing at first, particularly as there are several ways to go about it, but for all the projects in this book, every leg, arm and head begins with a Magic Ring, so you will soon have it mastered.

This is the method I use:

- Form a loop with the yarn, holding the loop in place using your fingers.

- Pass your hook through the loop (from front to back) and catch the working yarn with the hook.

- Draw the yarn back through the loop and make a chain stitch to secure the ring (this does not count as a stitch).

- Continue working stitches into the ring (and over the yarn tail) as instructed by the pattern.

- Pull on the yarn tail to draw the center of the loop closed.

Tip: To ensure the first stitch of the round is accessible, insert your hook into this stitch before drawing the center of the loop tightly closed. Work over the yarn tail for the first few stitches of the next round to make extra sure your Magic Ring stays tightly closed.

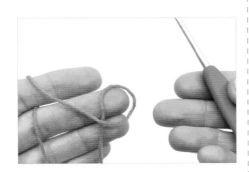

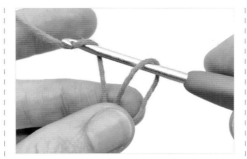

INVISIBLE DECREASE

Like the Magic Ring, the invisible decrease is another "must-have" in your amigurumi toolkit. As the name suggests, it creates a stitch that is virtually indistinguishable from a single crochet and eliminates the small gap left by a standard single crochet decrease. I recommend always using this technique when instructed to work a decrease (dec) stitch on a 3-dimensional piece (the back of an invisible decrease looks a little messy, so stick with a standard decrease when working in rows to create a flat piece).

- Insert hook under the **front loop** of the first stitch.

- Without yarning over, insert hook under the **front loop** of the next stitch.

- Yarn over and pull yarn through the 2 front loops (2 loops on hook).

- Yarn over and draw through both loops on hook.

V AND X SHAPED SINGLE CROCHET

In case you're just wrapping your head around the basic stitches, now I'm going to tell you there is more than one way to make a single crochet! The methods differ only in the direction that the yarn is wrapped around the crochet hook, but produce stitches that differ slightly in appearance. Depending on how you learnt to crochet, you may already be using one of several different variations.

Typically, the single crochet is worked as follows: insert hook into stitch, yarn over and pull yarn through stitch, yarn over and draw through both loops on hook. This creates a **V-shape** on the front of the stitch. However, if you replace the first yarn over with a **yarn under**, and otherwise complete the stitch in the same way, an **X-shaped** single crochet is formed (also referred to as **"cross stitch single crochet"**).

To complete a **yarn under**, position the hook behind the working space and catch the yarn from *above* (i.e., yarn **under** hook). By doing so, the legs of the stitch become partially crossed or twisted, rather than staying more parallel as with the traditional V-shaped single crochet.

Yarn over

Yarn Under

Comparison (YO vs YU)

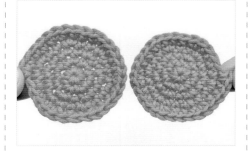

While this may seem like a subtle change, X-shaped single crochet forms a tighter stitch, and as such produces a slightly smaller crochet piece. As mentioned in *Working in the Round*, the way stitches stack when worked in the round means the start of the round shifts to the right as rounds are completed. X-shaped single crochet stitches do this to a lesser extent, which is why this method may be preferable if working with more complex color changes.

Having crocheted amigurumi projects using both methods, I now tend to favor the X-shaped single crochet and have worked all the dolls in the book this way. I love the look of the neat, compact stitches that this variation produces. However, the projects may be completed with either, so feel free to use the method to which you are accustomed.

COLOR CHANGES

Color changes are worked on the last step of the stitch **before** the indicated change. As you make the last stitch in the old color, drop the yarn to the back of the work and substitute with the new color for the final "yarn and draw through all loops on hook". The stitch is completed and the color changed in a single step. This produces a neater

change and the working loop on your hook is now in the new color, ready to continue.

Tip: Gently tug the loose ends to keep the stitch tension uniform.

COLOR WORK

Working multiple color changes, either across a round or over several rounds, can be used to create patterns and motifs on your amigurumi. The simplest example uses two colors worked in alternating rounds to create a horizontal stripe pattern. Color changes worked across a round may be represented in diagram form (in addition to the written pattern instructions), making the changes easier to visualize.

The technique for color work is the same as for a single color change, with the added consideration of how the different strands of color are carried through the work. In amigurumi, it is common to leave the "non-working" color at the back of the work, picking it up again before making the next color change. If the length of the color change is relatively short (no more than a few stitches), as is the case for the projects in this book, the non-working yarn can be left to strand (or float) across the backs of the stitches. It is important to ensure the strands are just loose enough to avoid distorting the crochet fabric.

STUFFING

"Stuff little and often" is a good guideline when working with amigurumi. Adding small wads of stuffing allows you to shape your amigurumi as you go, evenly distributing the fill to ensure a smooth finished toy. First separate a small clump of stuffing with your fingers and insert inside your crochet work, perhaps with the help of a stick of some description (I use a short wooden dowel or broken chopstick, very fancy).

Stuff firmly but not to the point that the fill places the crochet fabric under tension and holes appear between the stitches. At the same time, avoid under-stuffing as this can leave your doll looking a little sad and deflated! If you find the work becoming lumpy in sections, simply use your crochet hook to remove the

stuffing, fluff, and reinsert.

As my dolls are fairly small, I tend to stuff after completing each section, and provide prompts to do so in the written instructions for each pattern. The most important places to stuff firmly include the head and neck, as this will minimize the amount of head "wobble". To prevent the arms from sticking straight out from the sides of the body, I stuff only the lower portion, leaving the upper arm and "shoulder" unstuffed.

TENSION

Maintaining good stitch tension is important in amigurumi to avoid gaps in the work through which stuffing can show. This is done by balancing the force applied to the yarn by the hook, with the force applied by the hand controlling the yarn, as stitches are worked.

As discussed in **Crochet Hooks** on page 8, one way to improve stitch tension is to adjust the size of your crochet hook (select a smaller hook for tighter stitches). This is always preferable to modifying your crochet technique to work "extra-tight" stitches, which can lead to hand and wrist fatigue. If you do have a tendency to crochet with loose tension, consider adopting the X-shaped single crochet for your amigurumi, as this produces a more compact stitch.

Whatever your natural tension, try to be consistent; keeping your stitches the same size throughout will improve the overall appearance of your finished doll. Unfortunately I don't have any clever tips for improving stitch consistency, beyond simply "practice, practice, practice"!

Tip: "Gauge" is a term you will often see in knitting and crochet patterns, and it refers to the number of stitches and rows obtained per or inch (or centimeter). While gauge is important for garments or other fitted items, it is not so critical for amigurumi projects and I tend not to reference it in my patterns.

FASTENING OFF

When a section of crochet work is completed, the pattern will instruct you to **fasten off.** To do this, cut the yarn about 4" (10 cm) from the last stitch and expand the loop on your hook so the tail pulls through the stitch. If the work will be sewn onto an existing crochet piece, the pattern will specify to leave a **long yarn tail for sewing.** The length of the tail will depend on how many stitches you have to sew, but generally about 12-16" is sufficient (30-40 cm).

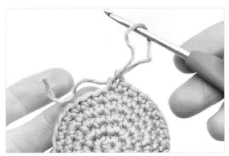

INVISIBLE FINISHES

Open Pieces
When fastening off an open piece worked in continuous rounds, you may wish to first work a slip stitch into the next stitch to minimize the jog in height. Alternatively, you can fasten off using an **invisible finish.** This technique creates a **"false stitch"** on top of the first stitch of the round, making the finish smoother and the edge stitches appear even.

- After fastening off, thread the tail onto a yarn needle.

- Skip the next (first) stitch and insert the needle into the second stitch of the round, from the front of the work to the back and under both loops (as you would your crochet hook).

- Next, insert the needle back down through the center of the last stitch of the round (i.e., through the back loop and back bar of the stitch the yarn tail is coming from) to complete the "false stitch".

- Tension the yarn so the size matches that of the surrounding stitches.

This same technique can be used when working in joined rounds (referred to as an **invisible join** or **needle join**), and replaces the traditional slip stitch join used to close a round.

Closed Pieces

When fastening off a closed piece, you will want to close the small hole left by the final round of stitches (usually about 6).

- After fastening off, thread the tail onto a yarn needle.

- Insert the needle under the front loop of the next stitch, from the front of the work to the back (as you would your crochet hook).

- Repeat for remaining stitches, inserting the needle under the front loop of each.

- Pull firmly on the yarn to close the hole.

- Insert the needle down through the middle of the closed hole, exiting the work some distance away, and pull yarn gently to create a smooth finish.

ATTACHING YARN

After fastening off, you may be required to **attach or join yarn** to a particular place on the crochet work, often to the first stitch (or turning chain) of a row or a previously unworked front loop. This can be done in a number of ways, the simplest of which is to insert your hook into the indicated stitch, pull up a loop of yarn, and make a chain stitch to secure (this does not count as a stitch). You now have a working loop on your hook ready to continue crocheting (be sure to **weave in** the starting yarn tail).

Alternatively, join the yarn using a **"standing single crochet"** by making a slip knot on your hook (acts as the working loop) before inserting the hook into the indicated stitch; yarn over and pull yarn through stitch (2 loops on hook), yarn over and draw through 2 loops on hook to complete the single crochet (counts as one stitch).

MANAGING YARN TAILS

Yarn tails not required for sewing must be hidden or secured within the work. If your doll is intended as a child's toy, you'll want to ensure yarn ends are well secured so the doll is sufficiently robust.

Hiding Ends

After fastening off an open 3-dimensional piece that will be crocheted to another section of the work, such as an arm or a leg, you may choose to simply tuck the yarn tail inside the piece. Subsequent joining rounds will ensure the end is secured within the doll.

Alternatively, you can work the next round or row over the yarn tail, securing it within the stitches. To do this, lay the tail along the top of the stitches to be worked and crochet over the strand for the next 3 or so stitches. This is a great option for color changes, or for doll clothing or other elements worked in rows, where you are moving back and forth from the location of the yarn end.

If all else fails, you will need to weave in the ends.

Weaving in Ends on a Flat Piece

Thread the tail onto a yarn needle and weave through the backs of several stitches, in several directions, on the wrong side of the work. Cut the yarn tail close to the surface of the work.

Weaving in Ends on a 3-dimensional Piece

Thread the tail onto a yarn needle and insert the needle all the way through the stuffed crochet piece, coming out between stitches some distance away and on the opposite side of the work. I like to repeat this several times, reinserting the needle back into the gap from which it existed each time and coming out again in a different location. To finish, pull gently on the tail and cut the yarn close to the surface of the work. Squeeze the crochet piece to retract the yarn end back inside the work, or use your yarn needle to assist.

SEWING, EMBROIDERY AND OTHER EMBELLISHMENTS

SEWING

Much like weaving in ends, sewing pieces of crochet together is rarely a crocheter's favorite task. Never fear, it's not mine either and I tend to design my dolls with this in mind. Here is some guidance for those places where a little sewing is required.

1. Body to Head

Use a yarn needle (blunt tip) and the yarn tail from the body. Position the neck opening over the joining round of the head. Sew around the neck, working stitches into both the back and front sides of the head, keeping the neck open and rounded.

- Insert yarn needle into a stitch on the back of the head, bringing the needle out one stitch along. *(image 1)*

- Insert needle under both loops of the next stitch on neck opening, from the back of the work to the front. *(image 2)*

- Reinsert needle back into the same stitch on the head from which you exited *(image 3)* and repeat the process, bringing the needle out one stitch along on the head and inserting it under both loops of the next stitch on the neck opening. *(image 4)*

- After 2 to 3 stitches, pull yarn firmly to draw the neck and head together, making the joining stitches almost invisible. *(image 5)*

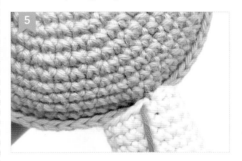

- Continue in this way, working all the way round the neck opening and pulling the stitches tight as you go. *(images 6-12)*

Sewing the head can take a little practice. Don't be afraid to remove stitches and start over if you're not completely happy with how your doll is looking.

2. Hair (or Hood) to Head

With the exception of "Amity", the hair (or hood) for my dolls are crocheted as one or two separate pieces and sewn on. These pieces

are worked in rows, beginning with either a magic ring or foundation chain, depending on the design.

Consistent stitch tension comes into play when fitting the hair to the front of the head. If the fit is firm (and it should be a little firm), gently ease the hair into position, ensuring it fits the full length of the **hairline**. You may find it helpful to use dress-making pins to secure the hair into place as you go. If the hair is too large, try reworking it with a hook half a millimeter smaller to see if you get a better result.

Using a yarn needle, work into the row ends (or back of the foundation chain) of the hair and into each stitch along the length of the **hairline**. I use a very basic method of sewing, just passing the needle through the crochet fabric and along to the next stitch, as you would for a simple **running stitch**. You could also use **whip stitch** here, if you prefer.

*Tip: The **hairline** refers to the section of the head joining round worked in hair colour.*

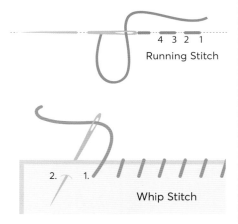

3. **Appliqué and Small Parts**
Attaching small crochet elements to your amigurumi is a great way to introduce a contrasting color or texture and create visual interest. Examples include flat appliqué, such as rosy-cheeks or pockets, or other design elements, such as ears or wings. I usually use one of two basic sewing methods, depending on whether I want the appliqué (or part) to blend into the surface on which it is

being sewn *(whip stitch)* or to have a more defined border *(running stitch)*.

To start, thread the yarn tail from the appliqué onto a yarn needle. Place the appliqué in position on your crochet work (secure with pins if required).

Whip stitch
From a stitch on the edge of the appliqué, insert the yarn needle under a loop directly beneath it on the crochet fabric (working away from the appliqué). *(image 1)* Insert the needle into the next stitch on the appliqué, from the front of the work to the back, and again under a loop directly beneath it on the crochet fabric. *(image 1 & 3)* Repeat until sewing is complete. *(image 4)*

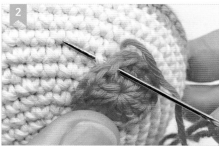

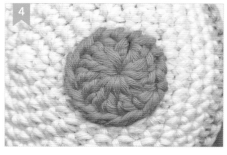

Running Stitch

From a stitch on the edge of the appliqué, insert the yarn needle under a loop directly beneath it on the crochet fabric. Bring the needle up through the next stitch on the appliqué, from the back of the work to the front. *(image 1)* Reinsert the needle back down through the appliqué in the next stitch along (from front to back) and again under a loop directly beneath it on the crochet fabric. *(image 2)* Repeat until sewing is complete. *(image 3 & 4)*

EMBROIDERY

I love adding simple embroidered elements to my crochet work; it's a great way to incorporate small details into the design and allows you, as the maker, to create something truely unique. Familiarity with a few basic stitches is all you need to get started.

Straight stitch

Bring threaded needle up from wrong to right side of fabric at the position you want to start the stitch. Insert the needle back into the fabric at the position you want to end the stitch. Repeat for the remaining stitches.

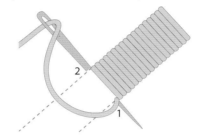

Fly stitch

Bring threaded needle up at point A, down at point B, and back up at point C (below and between A and B). Before tightening the working thread, loop it under the needle, creating a V-shaped stitch (with the thread hanging below). Complete either a V or Y shaped variation by bringing the thread down at, or some distance below, point C.

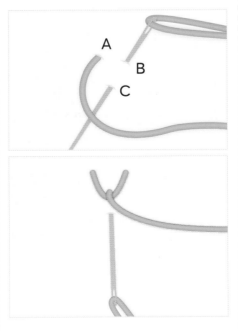

French Knot

Bring threaded needle up from wrong to right side of fabric at the position where you want the knot (#1). Wrap the yarn/thread twice around needle. Insert the needle back through the fabric, close to where it came up (almost in the same hole as #1). Gently pull the needle and yarn/thread through the wrapped loops to form the knot.

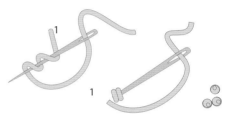

Face Embroidery

Embroidering the face on your amigurumi can take practice and patience, but always adds lots of individual personality to your doll. No two are ever the same! As you may discover, small changes in shape and placement can dramatically alter the appearance of the doll. The eyes and eyebrows, in particular, are defining features of any doll.

For the eyes, some of my favourites styles include **happy eyes** with up upward arc, **calm or bashful eyes** with a downward arc, or very simple **open eyes** made with of a few short, vertical straight stitches. You may, of course, determine the personality and mood of your doll by varying the facial features to suit. I encourage you to persevere until you have the look you're after, even if that means removing stitches and starting over. It will be worth it! Personally, I still find this task a little fiddly and time consuming, and rarely (actually, never) get it "right" first time.

Here are my top tips:

- For the projects in this book, I prefer to add the face after finishing the head and hair of the doll, to ensure correct placement.

- You may find it helpful to use dress-making pins to mark the positions of facial features before starting your embroidery.

- Use separate lengths of embroidery floss for each of the eyes and mouth. This way stitches can be easily removed from a particular feature that may need adjusting.

- For finer features, split the embroidery floss and remove one or two strands. To do this, separate the individual strands using your fingers and gently pull the strands apart. (image 1)

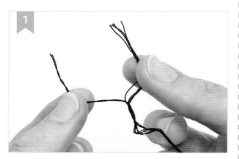

- Use an embroidery needle (sharp tip) and work *into* (rather than between) the stitches in the crochet fabric. This makes for more secure and precise stitch placement.

For **happy** or **bashful eyes**, I like to use the eyelashes to form the arc of the eyelid. This is the method I use:

- Thread needle with a length of embroidery floss of desired thickness.

- To start, insert embroidery needle into the crochet work on the back the head (between stitches), close to where you will be working. (image 2)

- Bring the needle up through a stitch on the face on the edge of the eye and insert back into the face at the opposite edge. (image 3)

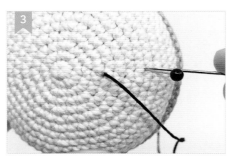

- Bring the needle up in the center of where the arc of the eyelid will be (either above the starting stitches for happy eyes (image 4) or below the starting stitches for bashful eyes), leaving a loose strand of thread on the surface of the work.

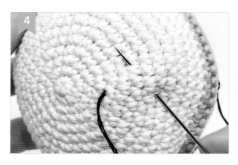

- Catch the strand (image 5) and reinsert needle a short distance away to form the first lash. (image 6)

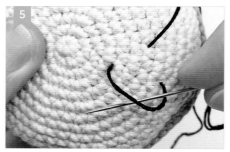

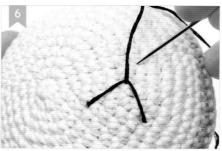

- Bring the needle back up on the arc in the location of the next lash. (image 7)

- Use the eye of the needle to slide under the arc of the eye and catch the strand (images 8 & 9), then reinsert needle a short distance away to form the eyelash, bringing the needle back up on the arc in the location of the next lash. (image 10)

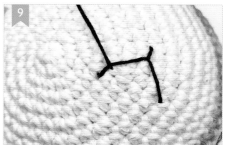

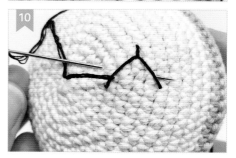

- Repeat this process across the arc of the eye, making about 5 evenly spaced lashes in total. (image 11-14)

- When finished, pass the needle back through the head, exiting between the same two stitches you started from. *(image 15)*

- Securely knot the start and end of the thread together and cut the thread a short distance from the knot. *(image 16)* Squeeze the work so the knot retracts inside the head, or use the tip of your scissors to push the knot to the inside. For extra security, leave a longer tail of thread and weave in the tail after knotting.

- For the **mouth**, I like to use just a simple a V-shaped **fly stitch**. *(image 17-19)*

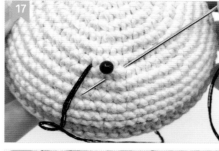

OTHER EMBELLISHMENTS

Surface crochet

Surface crochet refers to working stitches through the "fabric" of your crochet work, rather than across the top of the previous row or round. Most commonly applied using slip stitches on a flat crochet piece (or an open 3-dimensional piece for which you have access to the back of the work), this technique creates a neat chain across the surface of the fabric and is great for adding small extra details to your doll or their accessories.

Step 1: Insert your hook through the crochet fabric, from the front of the work to the back, in the location you wish to start your surface stitches.

Step 2: Holding the yarn at the back of the work, pull a loop of yarn up through the fabric. *(image 1)*

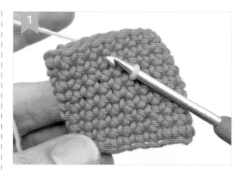

Step 3: Insert hook into the next stitch or space. *(image 2)*

Step 4: With the working yarn still at the back of the work, yarn over and draw the yarn through the work and the loop on the hook to complete a slip stitch. *(image 3)*

Step 5: Repeat Steps 3 and 4 as many times as required. *(image 4)*

Surface crochet can also be adapted for working on closed pieces, however as the working yarn must be kept at the front of the work (and therefore carried across the tops of the surface stitches), a small ridge is created. While the finish is not quite as neat, this modification does allow you to work with taller stitches and is great for creating texture or a sharp change in direction on the surface if your amigurumi.

Basic Crochet Cord

My favorite method for creating bag straps, handles and other doll accessories is with a simple crochet cord (also known as Romanian Cord). It's made using only single crochet stitches but produces a lovely texture that is the same on both sides. The technique starts with two set-up stitches and then uses a single stitch repeat until the cord is the desired length.

Step 1: Chain 2, single crochet in back loop of the first chain stitch after the slip knot. *(image 1)*

Step 2: Rotate work clockwise to insert hook down through the front loop of the second chain stitch after the slip knot. *(image 2)* Yarn over and pull yarn through loop (2 loops on hook). *(image 3)* Yarn over again and draw through both loops on hook to complete a single crochet. *(image 4)*

Step 3: Rotate work clockwise to insert hook down through the two horizontal strands at the base of the loop on the hook. *(image 5)* Yarn over and pull yarn through the two strands (2 loops on hook). *(image 6)* Yarn over again and draw through both loops on hook to complete a single crochet. *(image 7)*

Note: The two horizontal strands are the two loops through which the yarn was drawn to complete the previous single crochet.

Step 4: Repeat Step 3 until desired length is reached. *(image 8)*

ABBREVIATIONS AND TERMINOLOGY

The projects in this book use US crochet terminology.

BASIC CONVERSION CHART

US	UK
slip stitch (sl st)	slip stitch (sl st)
chain (ch)	chain (ch)
single crochet (sc)	double crochet (dc)
double crochet (dc)	treble crochet (tr)
half-double crochet (hdc)	half treble (htr)
treble (triple) crochet (tr)	double treble (dtr)

ABBREVIATIONS OF THE BASIC STITCHES

st(s)	Stitch(es)
ch	Chain Stitch
sl st	Slip Stitch
sc	Single Crochet Stitch
hdc	Half-Double Crochet Stitch
dc	Double Crochet Stitch
tr	Treble (or Triple) Crochet Stitch

CONCISE ACTION TERMS

dec	Decrease (work two or more stitches together)
inc	Increase (work two or more stitches into the same stitch)
join	Join two stitches together, usually with a slip stitch (either to complete the end of a closed round or when introducing a new ball or color of yarn)
turn	Turn your crochet piece horizontally to start the next row/round
yo	Yarn over (wrap the yarn over the hook)

STANDARD SYMBOLS USED IN PATTERNS

[ ]	Work instructions within brackets by the number of times indicated
( )	Work instructions within parentheses in the same stitch (or space) indicated

Projects

Ruby

The Grapefruit Girl

About 6¾" (17 cm) tall

MATERIALS & TOOLS

YARN: HELLO Cotton

Main color (MC): Misty Rose (163)
for Face, Arms & Legs

Color A: Nectarine (115)
for Hair (back of Head) & Shorts

Color B: Apricot (110)
for T-Shirt (Body)

Color C: Berry (108) for Hair

Color D: White (154)
for Hair Band & Shorts

Color E: Dark Salmon (112) for Cheeks

Color F: Ginger Root (165) for Basket

HOOK SIZE: 2.5 mm hook

OTHER: DMC Embroidery Floss - Black
for Eyes and Mouth

Embroidery Needle

Stitch Marker

Yarn Needle

Stuffing

Straight Pins

SPECIAL STITCHES & TECHNIQUES

Single Crochet Spike Stitch (sc-sp)

Insert hook in specified stitch one round below current round, pull up loop to height of stitches in current round, yarn over and draw through both loops on hook. (single crochet spike stitch made)

Double Crochet Decrease (dc-dec)

Yarn over and insert hook in stitch or space specified, pull up a loop (3 loops on hook), yarn over and draw through two loops on hook (2 loops remain on hook); yarn over, insert hook in next stitch or space and pull up a loop (4 loops on hook), yarn over and draw through two loops on hook (3 loops remain on hook). Yarn over and draw through all three loops on hook. (double crochet decrease made)

RUBY

HEAD

Front (Face)

Round 1: With MC, make a magic ring, 6 sc in ring. (6 sc)

Round 2: Inc in each st around. (12 sc)

Round 3: [Sc in next st, inc in next st] 6 times. (18 sc)

Round 4: [Sc in next st, inc in next st, sc in next st] 6 times. (24 sc)

Round 5: [Sc in each of next 3 sts, inc in next st] 6 times. (30 sc)

Round 6: [Sc in each of next 2 sts, inc in next st, sc in each of next 2 sts] 6 times. (36 sc)

Round 7: [Sc in each of next 5 sts, inc in next st] 6 times. (42 sc)

Round 8: [Sc in each of next 3 sts, inc in next st, sc in each of next 3 sts] 6 times. (48 sc)

Round 9: [Sc in each of next 7 sts, inc in next st] 6 times. (54 sc)

Round 10: [Sc in each of next 4 sts, inc in next st, sc in each of next 4 sts] 6 times. (60 sc)

Round 11: [Sc in each of next 9 sts, inc in next st] 6 times. (66 sc)

Rounds 12-13: *(2 rounds)* Sc in each st around. (66 sc)

Fasten off.

Back (Hair)

Rounds 1-12: *(12 Rounds)* With Color A, repeat Rounds 1-12 of Head Front (omitting Round 13). Do not fasten off. Continue with Head Assembly.

Head Assembly

1. Hold the Front and Back together with right sides facing outwards.

2. With Color A, single crochet in both the next stitch on Back and corresponding stitch on Front. *(image 1)* This is the first stitch of the "Hairline".

3. Working through both Back and Front together, single crochet in each of next 50 stitches to complete the Hairline. (51 stitches) *(image 2)*

4. Change to MC, and continue working single crochet stitches, stuffing the Head firmly before finishing the round. *(image 3)*

5. Join the round with a slip stitch in the first single crochet stitch.

6. Fasten off and weave in ends.

7. Set Head aside.

ARM (Make 2)

Round 1: With MC, make a magic ring, 6 sc in ring. (6 sc)

Round 2: Inc in each st around. (12 sc)

Rounds 3-4: *(2 rounds)* Sc in each st around. (12 sc)

Round 5: Sc in each of next 6 sts, [dec] 3 times. (9 sc)

Rounds 6-11: *(6 rounds)* Sc in each st around. (9 sc)

Round 12: Sc in each of next 5 sts, change to Color B, sc in each of next 4 sts. (9 sc)

Rounds 13-14: *(2 rounds)* With Color B, sc in each st around. (9 sc)

Round 15: Dec, sc in each of next 7 sts. (8 sc)

Row 16: Sc in each of next 3 sts. *(This positions the decreases from Round 5 to the outer Arm.)* *(image 4)*

Fasten off.

1. Stuff the lower third of each Arm, leaving the remainder of Arm unstuffed.

2. Set Arms aside.

LEGS & BODY

First Leg

Round 1: With MC, make a magic ring, 6 sc in ring. (6 sc)

Round 2: Inc in each st around. (12 sc)

Rounds 3-10: *(8 rounds)* Sc in each st around. (12 sc)

Round 11: Change to Color A, sc in each st around. (12 sc)

Row 12: Sc-sp in each of next 11 sts. (11 sts)

Do not work last st.

Fasten off.

Second Leg

Rounds 1-11: *(11 rounds)* With MC, repeat Rounds 1-11 of First Leg.

Round 12: Sc-sp in each st around. (12 sts)

Row 13: Sc in next st. Do not fasten off. Continue with Body.

Body

Round 1: *(Joining Legs)* From Second Leg, ch 3; working on First Leg, sc in next st *(unspiked st on Round 11)*, sc in each of next 11 sts; working in ch-3, sc in each of next 3 ch; working on Second Leg, sc in each of next 12 sts; working on other side of ch-3, sc in each of next 3 ch. (30 sc)

Round 2: Sc in each of next 6 sts, inc in next st, sc in each of next 14 sts, inc in next st, sc in each of next 8 sts. (32 sc)

Round 3: [Sc in each of next 3 sts, inc in next st] 8 times. (40 sc)

Stuff the Legs.

Rounds 4-8: *(5 rounds)* Sc in each st around. (40 sc)

Round 9: Sc in each of next 8 sts, dec, sc in each of next 18 sts, dec, sc in each of next 10 sts. (38 sc)

Change to Color B.

Round 10: Working in back loops only, sc in each of next 8 sts, dec, sc in each of next 17 sts, dec, sc in each of next 9 sts. (36 sc) *(image 5)*

Round 11: [Sc in each of next 4 sts, dec] 6 times. (30 sc)

Rounds 12-13: *(2 rounds)* Sc in each st around. (30 sc)

Round 14: [Sc in each of next 3 sts, dec] 6 times. (24 sc)

Round 15: Sc in each st around. (24 sc)

Start stuffing the Body.

Round 16: [Sc in each of next 4 sts, dec] 4 times. (20 sc)

Note: *When attaching each Arm, flatten the top of the Arm and hold against the Body with the decrease stitches on Round 5 facing outwards. (image 6) Work the "attaching" stitches through both the layers of the Arm and the Body together.*

Round 17: *(Attaching Arms)* Sc in each of next 4 sts; working on First Arm & Body, sc in each of next 4 sts *(image 7)* *(First Arm attached)*; working on Body only, sc in each of next 8 sts; working on Second Arm & Body, sc in each of next 4 sts *(Second Arm attached)*. (20 sc)

Round 18: Sc in each of next 4 sts, [dec] 2 times, sc in each of next 8 sts, [dec] 2 times. (16 sc)

Change to MC.

Round 19: *(Neck)* Sc in each st around. (16 sc)

Fasten off, leaving a long tail for sewing. *(image 8)*

1. Finish stuffing the Body.

2. Using long tail and yarn needle, sew Body to Head, working through all 16 sts around Neck.

TIP: *Ensure Body is centered between ends of Hairline. Maintain a wide, round Neck opening, adding extra stuffing before finishing.*

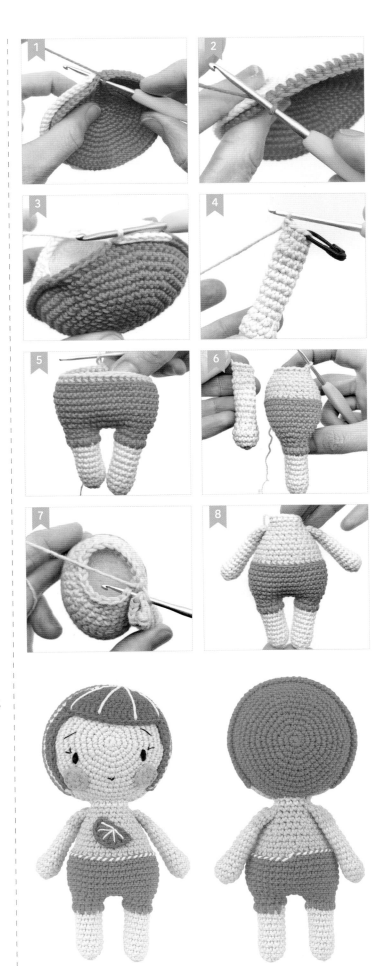

HAIR

Row 1: *(Wrong Side)* With Color C, make a magic ring, ch 3 *(counts as first dc, now and throughout)*, 5 dc in ring. (6 dc) Tighten ring but do not join round.

Row 2: *(Right Side)* Ch 3, turn, dc in first st, 2 dc in each of next 4 sts, 2 dc in last st *(3rd ch of ch-3)*. (12 dc)

Row 3: Ch 3, turn, dc in first st, [dc in next st, 2 dc in next st] 5 times, dc in last st. (18 dc)

Row 4: Ch 3, turn, dc in first st, dc in each of next 3 sts, 2 dc in next st, dc in each of next 8 sts, 2 dc in next st, dc in each of next 3 sts, 2 dc in last st. (22 dc) *(image 9)* Do not finish off.

First Side Piece: Ch 11, turn, *(image 10)*, sl st in 2nd ch from hook, sc in each of next 6 ch, dc in each of next 3 ch. (10 sts) *(image 11)* Sl st in 3rd st on Row 4 to join. *(image 12)* Fasten off.

Second Side Piece: With right side facing, attach Color C to first dc *(3rd ch of ch-3)* on Row 4 *(image 13)*, ch 16 *(image 14)*, sl st in 2nd ch from hook, sc in each of next 4 ch, [dc-dec *(using next 2 ch)*, dc in each of next 2 ch] 2 times, dc-dec *(using last 2 ch)*. (12 sts) *(image 15)* Sl st in 4th st on Row 4 to join. *(image 16)* Fasten off.

Hair Band *(Grapefruit Rind)*: With right side facing, working in other side of chain of First Side piece, attach Color D to first ch, sc in same first ch, sc in each of next 9 ch *(image 17)*; working in sides of rows, 2 sc in each of next 4 rows, sc in ring, 2 sc in each of next 4 rows, *(image 18)*; working in other side of ch on Second Side piece, sc in each of next 15 ch. *(image 19)* (42 sc) Fasten off.

Hair Edging *(Grapefruit Zest)*: With right side facing attach Color A to first st of Hair Band, sc in first st, sc in each of next 4 sts *(image 20)*, [inc in next st, sc in each of next 3 sts] 9 times, sc in last st. (51 sc) *(image 21)* Fasten off, leaving long tail for sewing.

1. Position the Hair on Head Front, gently shaping the Hair Edging along the Hairline, and securing with pins. *(image 22)*

2. Using the long tail and yarn needle, sew the Hair in place, matching the 51 stitches of the Hair Edging to the 51 stitches on the Hairline. *(image 23)*

FINISHING - Use photos as guide

Cheek (Make 2)

Round 1: With Color E, make a magic ring, ch 2 *(does not count as a stitch)*, 10 hdc in ring, join with sl st to first hdc. (10 hdc)

Fasten off, leaving long tail for sewing.

Facial Features

TIP: *Use straight pins to mark the positions of the desired facial features, or use photos as a guide. (image 24)*

1. Using the long tail and yarn needle, sew Cheeks to either side of Face, just inside ends of Hair.

2. With Black Floss (using 4 to 6 strands, depending on preferred thickness), embroider Mouth over Round 8.

3. For Eyes, make several vertical straight stitches over a height of 2 sc.

4. Use 2 strands of Floss to add eyelashes and eyebrows.

Hair

With Color D, embroider several long straight stitches across Hair Rows 1 to 4 to create grapefruit "segments", using photos as a guide. *(image 25)*

T-Shirt Appliqué

Row 1: With Color C, make a magic ring, ch 3, 10 dc in ring. Do not join. Tighten ring, arranging stitches to create a half-circle. Fasten off, leaving a long tail for sewing.

1. Split a length of yarn in Color D and using embroidery needle, add segment lines to the front of Row 1, using photos as a guide.

2. Position appliqué to front of Body, between Rounds 12 & 16. Using long tail and yarn needle, sew in place.

Belt

With Color D, use a yarn needle and weave yarn through unworked front loops from Round 9 of Body. *(images 26 & 27)* Weave in ends.

ACCESSORIES

Basket

Round 1: With Color F, make a magic ring, ch 1 *(does not count as a stitch, now and throughout)*, 8 hdc in ring; join with sl st to first hdc. (8 hdc)

Round 2: Ch 1, 2 hdc in same st as joining, 2 hdc in each of next 7 sts; join with sl st to first hdc. (16 hdc)

Round 3: Ch 1, hdc in same st as joining, 2 hdc in next st, [hdc in next st, 2 hdc in next st] 7 times; join with sl st to first hdc. (24 hdc) *(image 28)*

Round 4: Ch 1, working in back loops only, inc in same st as joining, sc in each of next 23 sts. (25 sc) Do not join.

Work in continuous rounds - without joining.

Round 5: Sc in next st, [sc in back loop of next st, sc-sp in next st] 12 times. (25 sts)

Round 6: [Sc in back loop of next st, sc-sp in next st] 12 times, sc in back loop of next st. (25 sts)

Round 7: [Sc-sp in next st, sc in back loop of next st] 12 times, sc-sp in next st. (25 sts) *(image 29)*

Round 8: Sc in back loop of next st, sc-sp in next st, ch 5, skip next 3 sts *(First Handle)*, sc-sp in next st, [sc in back loop of next st, sc-sp in next st] 4 times, ch 5, skip next 3 sts *(Second Handle)*, [sc-sp in next st, sc in back loop of next st] 4 times. (19 sts & 2 ch-5 loops)

Round 9: Sc-sp in next st, sc in back loop of next st, 5 sc in ch-5 sp, [sc in back loop of next st, sc-sp in next st] 4 times, sc in back loop of next st, 5 sc in ch-5 sp, [sc in back loop of next st, sc-sp in next st] 4 times. (29 sts) *(image 30)*

Round 10: Sl st in each st around. (29 sl st)

Fasten off and weave in ends.

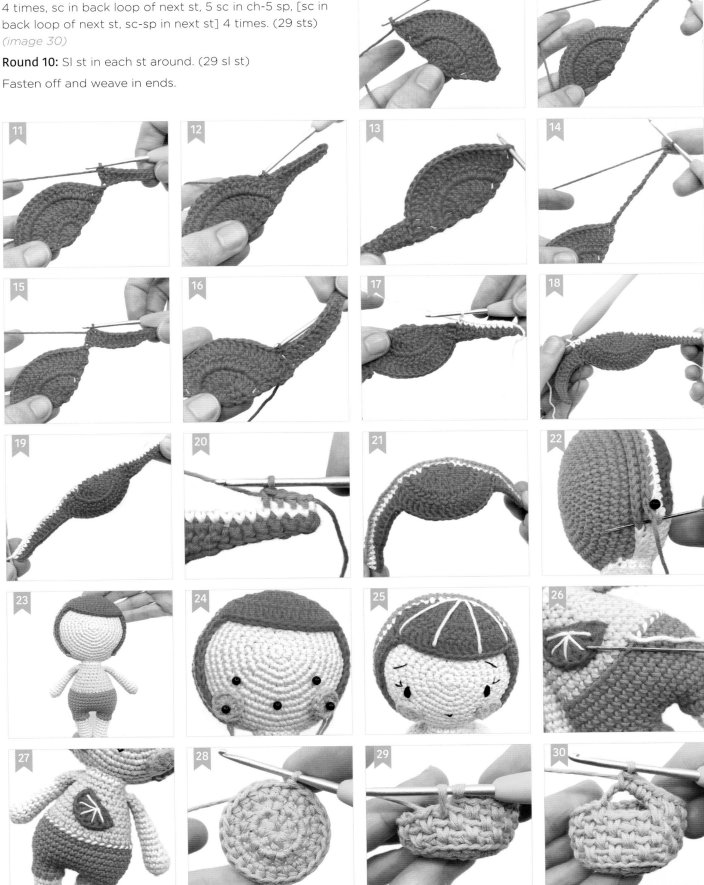

Amity the Adventurer

A Dress-Up Doll

About 8¾" (22 cm) tall

MATERIALS & TOOLS

YARN: HELLO Cotton

— **Main color (MC):** Misty Rose (163) for Face, Arms & Legs

— **Color A:** Rusty Brown (167) for Hair

— **Color B:** Salmon (109) for Bodysuit & Cheeks

HOOK SIZE: 2.5 mm hook

OTHER: DMC Embroidery Floss
   Black for Eyes and Mouth
   Embroidery Needle
   2 x Small Hair Elastics (optional)
   Blush & Makeup Brush (optional)
   Stitch Marker
   Yarn Needle
   Stuffing
   Straight Pins

SPECIAL STITCHES & TECHNIQUES

ATTACHING HAIR

1. Fold one strand of yarn in half, forming a loop. Insert hook in stitch specified and place loop on hook. *(image 1)*

2. Pull loop part-way through. *(image 2)*

3. Wrap both yarn ends over hook and draw them through loop. *(image 3)*

4. Tug ends gently to tighten knot. *(image 4)*

5. Repeat steps 1-4 in specified stitches as needed. *(image 5)*

AMITY DOLL

HEAD

Front (Face)

Round 1: With MC, make a magic ring, 6 sc in ring. (6 sc)

Round 2: Inc in each st around. (12 sc)

Round 3: [Sc in next st, inc in next st] 6 times. (18 sc)

Round 4: [Sc in next st, inc in next st, sc in next st] 6 times. (24 sc)

Round 5: [Sc in each of next 3 sts, inc in next st] 6 times. (30 sc)

Round 6: [Sc in each of next 2 sts, inc in next st, sc in each of next 2 sts] 6 times. (36 sc)

Round 7: [Sc in each of next 5 sts, inc in next st] 6 times. (42 sc)

Round 8: [Sc in each of next 3 sts, inc in next st, sc in each of next 3 sts] 6 times. (48 sc)

Round 9: [Sc in each of next 7 sts, inc in next st] 6 times. (54 sc)

Round 10: [Sc in each of next 4 sts, inc in next st, sc in each of next 4 sts] 6 times. (60 sc)

Round 11: [Sc in each of next 9 sts, inc in next st] 6 times. (66 sc)

Round 12: [Sc in each of next 5 sts, inc in next st, sc in each of next 5 sts] 6 times. (72 sc)

Rounds 13-14: *(2 rounds)* Sc in each st around. (72 sc)
Fasten off.

Back (Hair)

Rounds 1-13: *(13 Rounds)* With Color A, repeat Rounds 1-13 of Head Front (omitting Round 14). Do not fasten off. Continue with Head Assembly.

Head Assembly

1. Hold the Front and Back together with right sides facing outwards. *(image 6)*

2. With Color A, single crochet in both the next stitch on Back and corresponding stitch on Front. *(image 7)* This is the first stitch of the "Hairline".

3. Working through both Back & Front together, single crochet in each of next 53 stitches to complete the Hairline. (54 stitches) *(image 8)*

4. Change to MC, and continue working single crochet stitches, stuffing the Head firmly before finishing the round. *(image 9)*

5. Join the round with a slip stitch in the first single crochet stitch.

6. Fasten off and weave in ends. *(image 10)*

7. Set Head aside.

ARM (Make 2)

Round 1: With MC, make a magic ring, 5 sc in ring. (5 sc)

Round 2: Inc in each st around. (10 sc)

Rounds 3-20: *(18 rounds)* Sc in each st around. (10 sc)
Fasten off.

1. Stuff the lower half of each Arm, leaving the upper Arm unstuffed.

2. Set Arms aside.

LEGS & BODY

First Leg

Round 1: With MC, make a magic ring, 6 sc in ring. (6 sc)

Round 2: Inc in each st around. (12 sc)

Rounds 3-25: *(23 rounds)* Sc in each st around. (12 sc)
Fasten off.

Second Leg

Rounds 1-25: *(25 rounds)* With MC, repeat Rounds 1-25 of First Leg.

Change to Color B. Fasten off MC.

Stuff Legs firmly. Continue with Body.

Body

Round 1: *(Joining Legs)* From Second Leg, ch 3; working on First Leg, sc in next st *(first st of last round)* *(image 11)*, sc in each of next 11 sts; working in ch-3, sc in each of next 3 ch; working on Second Leg, sc in each of next 12 sts; working on other side of ch-3, sc in each of next 3 ch. (30 sc) *(image 12)*

Round 2: Sc in each of next 5 sts, inc in next st, sc in each of next 15 sts, inc in next st, sc in each of next 8 sts. (32 sc)

Round 3: [Sc in each of next 7 sts, inc in next st] 4 times. (36 sc)

Round 4: [Sc in each of next 4 sts, inc in next st, sc in each of next 4 sts] 4 times. (40 sc)

Rounds 5-8: *(4 rounds)* Sc in each st around. (40 sc)

Round 9: Sc in each of next 9 sts, dec, sc in each of next 18 sts, dec, sc in each of next 9 sts. (38 sc)

Round 10: Sc in each of next 9 sts, dec, sc in each of next 17 sts, dec, sc in each of next 8 sts. (36 sc)

Round 11: Sc in each st around. (36 sc)

Round 12: [Sc in each of next 4 sts, dec] 6 times. (30 sc)

Rounds 13-14: *(2 rounds)* Sc in each st around. (30 sc)

Round 15: [Sc in each of next 4 sts, dec] 5 times. (25 sc)

Round 16: Sc in each st around. (25 sc)

Start stuffing the Body.

Round 17: [Sc in each of next 3 sts, dec] 5 times. (20 sc)

Note: *When attaching each Arm, flatten the top of the Arm and hold against the Body. Work the "attaching" stitches through both the layers of the Arm and the Body together. (image 13)*

Round 18: *(Attaching Arms)* Sc in each of next 4 sts; working on First Arm & Body, sc in each of next 5 sts *(First Arm attached) (image 14)*; working on Body only, sc in each of next 6 sts; working on Second Arm & Body, sc in each of next 5 sts *(Second Arm attached)*. (20 sc) *(image 15)*

Round 19: Sc in each st around. (20 sc)

Change to MC.

Round 20: Sc in each of next 5 sts, [dec] 2 times, sc in each of next 7 sts, [dec] 2 times. (16 sc)

Round 21: *(Neck)* Sc in each st around. (16 sc)

Fasten off, leaving a long tail for sewing.

1. Finish stuffing the Body.

2. Using long tail and yarn needle, sew Body to Head, working through all 16 sts around Neck. *(images 16-19)*

TIP: *Ensure Body is centered between ends of Hairline. Maintain a wide, round Neck opening, adding extra stuffing before finishing.*

HAIR

Using Color A, cut approximately 64 yarn strands, 14" (36 cm) each in length.

1. Mark the center point of the forehead on Round 10 of Head Front. *(image 20)*

2. Starting at marked point, attach Hair strand to the 16 stitches on either side of this point, inserting the hook from right to left around each stitch. (Using the smaller hook is optional but recommended.) *(image 21)*

3. From the last knot on either side, continue attaching Hair strands (about 2 or 3 knots per round for coverage),

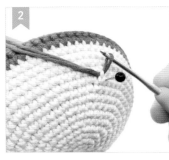
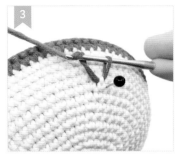
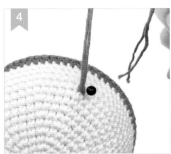

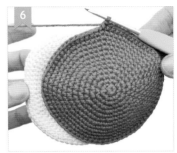

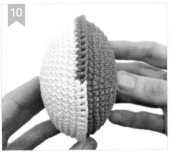

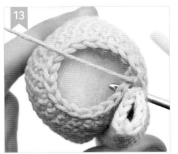

tapering them across Rounds 11 to 14 to meet at the end of the Hairline on both sides. *(image 22)*

4. At the crown, behind the marked point, attach about 4 Hair strands on each of Rounds 11 to 14. *(image 23)*

5. Gather Hair in two sections and fasten with hair elastics or yarn scraps. *(image 24)* Trim to neaten the ends.

Note: For more hair coverage (which allows for more styling options), cut additional long yarn strands and fill in remaining spaces, as desired. (image 25)

Hair Bangs

Using Color A, cut 22 strands, 8" (20 cm) each in length.

1. Using the same technique, but inserting hook from the top to the bottom of each stitch *(image 26)*, attach yarn strands to Round 9 of Head Front (11 sts on either side of marked point) so the strands hang over the Face.

2. Trim the Bangs to neaten ends, and style as desired.

FACE - Use photos as guide

TIP: Use straight pins to mark the positions of the desired facial features. The Mouth is centered on Round 9. The base of the Eyes are positioned about 6 stitches away on either side of Mouth position. (image 27)

1. With Black Floss (using 4 to 6 strands, depending on preferred thickness), embroider Mouth.

2. For the Eyes, make several vertical straight stitches over a height of 2 sc. *(image 28)*

3. Use 2 strands of Floss to add eyelashes and eyebrows. *(image 29)*

4. With Color B and yarn needle, embroider a few short, straight stitches under the outer edge of each Eye, to add Cheek markings. For extra rosy cheeks, add a light dusting of blush (optional). *(image 30)*

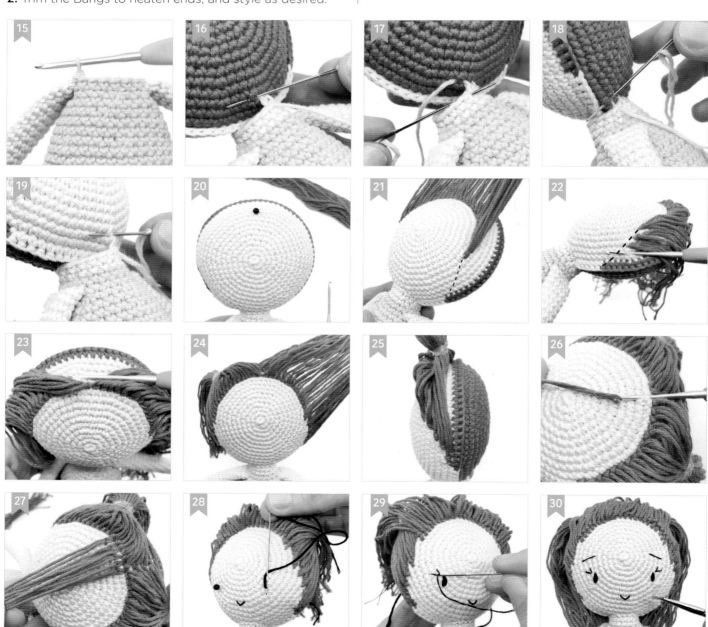

40

Amity's

OCEAN ADVENTURE OUTFIT

MATERIALS & TOOLS

YARN: HELLO Cotton

- **Color A:** Red (114) for Shorts
- **Color B:** White (154) for Shorts
- **Color C:** Baby Blue (146) for Mask
- **Color D:** Grey Blue (149) for Snorkel
- **Color E:** Golden Yellow (121) for Fins

HOOK SIZE: 3.0 mm hook
2.5 mm hook for Fins & Snorkel

OTHER: Stitch Markers
Yarn Needle

SWIM SHORTS

Note: *Shorts are worked from the bottom up.*

Leg Openings: With Color A and larger hook, ch 15; taking care not to twist ch, join with sl st in first ch to form a ring *(First Leg)* *(image 1)*; ch 16 *(image 2)*, taking care not to twist ch, sl st in 15th ch from hook *(Second Leg)*, sc in next ch st *(center stitch)* *(image 3)*. (2 ch-15 loops, 1 sc)

Round 1: Working around First Leg, sc in first ch *(same ch as sl st)*, sc in each of next 6 ch, inc in next ch, sc in each of next 7 ch *(image 4)*; sc in other side of center stitch; working around Second Leg, sc in first ch *(same ch as sl st)*, sc in each of next 6 ch, inc in next ch, sc in each of next 7 ch; sc in center stitch. *(image 5)* (34 sc - *16 sts around each Leg + 1 sc on either side of center st*)

Change to Color B.

Continue in a stripe pattern, alternating Color B and Color A each round.

Round 2: *(Color B)* Working in back loops only, sc in each of next 8 sts, inc in next st, sc in each of next 16 sts, inc in next st, sc in each of next 8 sts. (36 sc)

Round 3: *(Color A)* Working in back loops only, sc in each st around. (36 sc)

Round 4: *(Color B)* Working in back loops only, [sc in each of next 8 sts, inc in next st] 4 times. (40 sc)

Round 5: *(Color A)* Working in back loops only, sc in each st around. (40 sc)

Round 6: *(Color B)* Working in back loops only, sc in each st around. (40 sc)

Change to Color A.

Round 7: Working in back loops only, [sc in each of next 8 sts, dec] 4 times. (36 sc)

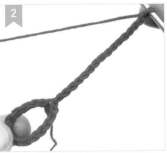
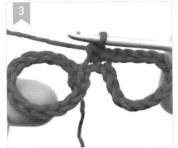

Round 8: Working in back loops only, sl st in each st around. (36 sl sts)

Fasten off and weave in ends. *(image 6)*

MASK

Row 1: *(Right Side)* With Color C and larger hook, ch 15, sc in 2nd ch from hook, sc in each of next 13 ch. (14 sc)

Row 2: Ch 1, turn, inc in first st, sc in each of next 12 sts, inc in last st. (16 sc)

Rows 3-5: *(3 rows)* Ch 1, turn, sc in each st across. (16 sc)

Row 6: Ch 1, turn, sc in each of next 7 sts. (7 sc) Leave remaining stitches unworked.

Row 7: Ch 1, turn, skip first st, sc in each of next 6 sts. (6 sc)

Row 8: Ch 1, turn, skip first st, sc in each of next 5 sts. (5 sc)

Row 9: Ch 1, turn, skip first st, sc in each of next 3 sts, inc in last st. (5 sc)

Edging: Ch 1 *(do not turn)* *(image 7)*; working in sides of rows, skip 2 rows, sc in each of next 6 rows *(image 8)*, inc in last row *(corner)*; working on other side of starting ch, skip first ch, sc in each of next 12 ch, skip last ch *(image 9)*; working in sides of rows, inc in first row, sc in each of next 3 rows.

Remove hook and place marker in working loop.

Cut yarn, leaving a 16" (40 cm) tail. *(image 10)*

Row 6a: With wrong side facing, working in remaining sts on Row 5, skip next 2 sts, attach Color C in next st *(image 11)*, sc in same st, sc in each of next 6 sts. (7 sc)

Row 7a: Ch 1, turn, sc in each of next 5 sts, dec *(using last 2 sts)*. (6 sc)

Row 8a: Ch 1, turn, skip first st, sc in each of next 5 sts. (5 sc)

Row 9a: Ch 1, turn, sc in each st across. (5 sc) *(image 12)*

Bridge Edging: Do not turn; working in sides of rows, skip first row, sc in each of next 3 rows; working in Row 5, sc in each of 2 skipped sts; working in sides of rows, sc in each of next 3 rows, skip last row; join with a sl st in next st *(first st of Row 9)*. *(image 13)* Fasten off.

Finish Edging: Insert hook in marked working loop *(image 14)* and sc in each of next 3 rows; join with sl st in next st *(first st of Row 9a)*.

Fasten off and weave in ends.

Mask Trim: With Color A, attach yarn to any stitch on edge of Mask. Sl st in each st around. Fasten off and weave in ends. *(image 15)*

Strap

Note: *If preferred, work 30 Foundation Half-Double Crochets (or to desired length).*

With Color A, ch 32; hdc in 3rd ch from hook, hdc in remaining 29 ch. (30 hdc)

Fasten off, leaving a long tail for sewing.

1. Using long tail and yarn needle, secure one end of Strap to side of Mask (between Rounds 4 & 5).

2. Cut a strand of Color A and sew the other end of Strap to the other side of Mask. Weave in all ends.

SNORKEL

Round 1: With Color D and smaller hook, make a magic ring; 7 sc in ring. (7 sc)

Round 2: Inc in each st around. (14 sc)

Round 3: [Sc in next st, inc in next st] 7 times. (21 sc) *(image 16)*

Round 4: Skip next 13 sts, sc in next st *(folding circle)*; *(image 17)*, sc in each of next 7 sts. (8 sc)

Rounds 5-15: *(11 rounds)* Sc in each st around. (8 sc) *(image 18)*

Fasten off and weave in ends.

Round 4a: Working in skipped sts on Round 3, attach Color D to 3rd st *(image 19)*, sl st in each of next 8 sts. (8 sl sts) Leave remaining sts unworked.

Fasten off, leaving a long tail for sewing.

1. Use the long tail and yarn needle, sew the 2 skipped stitches at the beginning of Round 4a to the 2 unworked stitches at the end of the round. *(images 20 & 21)*

2. Sew the Snorkel securely to the Mask Strap at the side of the Mask. *(image 22)*

FIN (Make 2)

Leg Opening: With Color E and smaller hook, ch 16; taking care not to twist ch, join with sl st in first ch to form a ring.

Round 1: Ch 1, sc in each ch around. (16 sc)

Work in continuous rounds - without joining.

Rounds 2-5: *(4 rounds)* Sc in each st around. (16 sc)

Round 6: [Sc in each of next 2 sts, dec] 4 times. (12 sc)

Round 7: Sc in each st around. (12 sc) *(image 23)*

Round 8: Sc in each of next 2 sts, inc in next st, sc in each of next 9 sts. (13 sc)

Round 9: Sc in each of next 9 sts, inc in next st, sc in each of next 3 sts. (14 sc)

Round 10: Sc in each st around. (14 sc)

Round 11: Sc in each of next 3 sts, inc in next st, sc in each of next 10 sts. (15 sc)

Round 12: Sc in each of next 12 sts, inc in next st, sc in each of next 2 sts. (16 sc)

Rounds 13-22: *(10 rounds)* Sc in each st around. (16 sc)

Fasten off, leaving a long tail for sewing.

1. Use long tail and yarn needle to whip stitch across flattened last round. *(images 24 & 25)*

Dress Amity in her snorkeling gear ready for her ocean adventure!

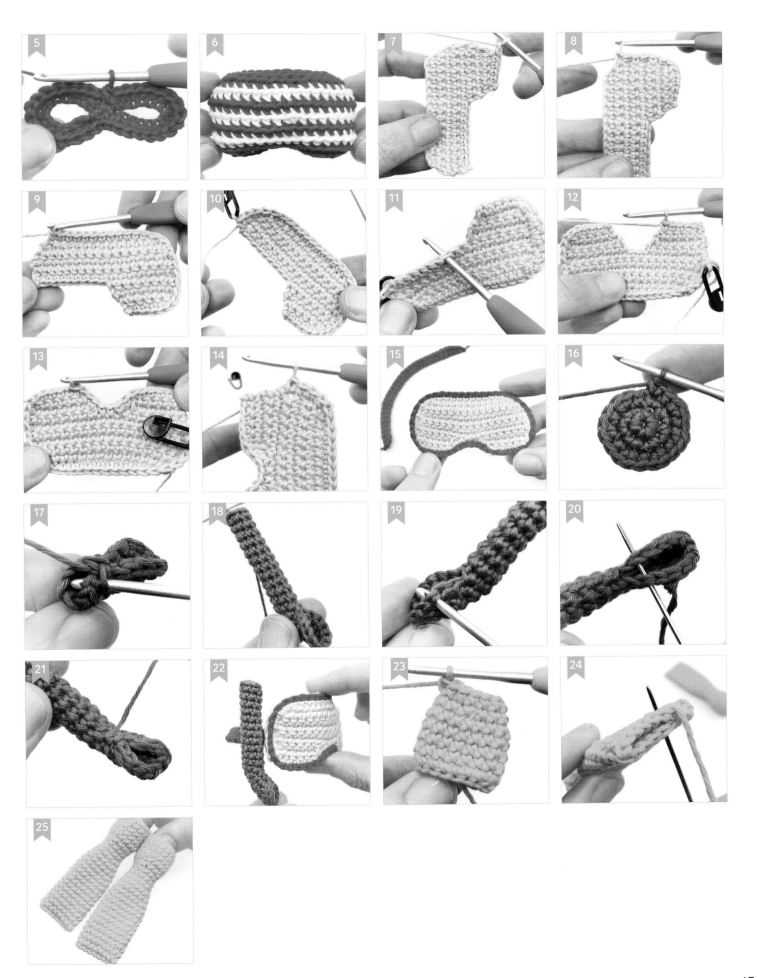

Amity's

COOKING ADVENTURE OUTFIT

MATERIALS & TOOLS

YARN: HELLO Cotton

- **Color A:** White (154) for Chef Hat & Pants
- **Color B:** Pink (103) for Jacket
- **Color C:** Black (160) for Pants & Shoes
- **Color D:** Cream (156) for Bowl
- **Color E:** Russet (168) for Spoon
- Small amount of Doll's Hair Color for Hat Strap

HOOK SIZE: 3.0 mm hook - Main hook
2.5 mm hook - for Pants & Shoes
2.0 mm hook - for Accessories

OTHER: DMC Embroidery Floss - Black for Jacket buttons
Embroidery Needle
Small Snap Fastener for Chef Jacket
Stitch Marker
Yarn Needle

SPECIAL STITCHES & TECHNIQUES

Single Crochet Decrease over 3 Stitches (3-dec)

*Insert hook in next stitch and pull up a loop; repeat from * 2 times more (4 loops on hook); yarn over and draw through all 4 loops. (decrease made)

Single Crochet Spike Stitch (sc-sp)

Insert hook in specified stitch one round below current round, pull up loop to height of stitches in current round, yarn over and draw through both loops on hook. (single crochet spike stitch made)

COOKING OUTFIT

CHEF HAT

Round 1: With Color A and main hook, make a magic ring; 8 sc in ring. (8 sc)

Round 2: Inc in each st around. (16 sc)

Round 3: Inc in each st around. (32 sc)

Round 4: [Sc in next st, inc in next st] 16 times. (48 sc) *(image 1)*

Rounds 5-6: *(2 rounds)* Sc in each st around. (48 sc)

Round 7: [Dec, sc in next st] 16 times. (32 sc)

Round 8: [Sc in next st, dec, sc in next st] 8 times. (24 sc)

Round 9: [Dec, sc in each of next 2 sts] 6 times. (18 sc)

Round 10: Working in back loops only, sc in each st around. (18 sc)

Rounds 11-12: *(2 rounds)* Sc in each st around. (18 sc)

Fasten off and weave in ends.

Hat Strap: Using about 12" (30 cm) length of Hair Color yarn, tie each end to either side of last round on Hat, adjusting to fit. *(image 2)*

Note: *With the Hat in position, the Hat Strap fits down and around the back of the Head.*

JACKET

Note: *Jacket is worked from top down.*

Row 1: *(Right Side)* With Color B and main hook, ch 25, sc in 2nd ch from from hook, sc in each of next 23 ch. (24 sc)

Row 2: Ch 1, turn, sc in first st, sc in each of next 2 sts, ch 5, skip next 4 sts *(First Armhole)*, sc in each of next 6 sts, ch 5, skip next 4 sts *(Second Armhole)*, sc in each of next 7 sts. (16 sc & 2 ch-5 loops)

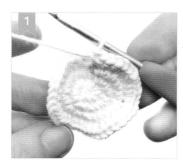

Row 3: Ch 1, turn, sc in first st, sc in each of next 6 sts; working in ch-5, sc in each of next 5 ch; inc in next st, sc in each of next 4 sts, inc in next st; working in ch-5, sc in each of next 5 ch; sc in each of next 3 sts. (28 sc) *(image 3)*

Row 4: Ch 1, turn, [sc in each of next 3 sts, inc in next st] 7 times. (35 sc)

Row 5: Ch 1, turn, sc in each st across. (35 sc)

Row 6: Ch 1, turn, [sc in each of next 3 sts, inc in next st, sc in each of next 3 sts) 5 times. (40 sc)

Rows 7-8: *(2 rows)* Sc in each st across. (40 sc)

Row 9: Ch 1, turn, inc in first st, sc in each of next 39 sts. (41 sc)

Row 10: Ch 1, turn, [sc in each of next 7 sts, inc in next st] 4 times, sc in each of next 9 sts. (45 sc)

Rows 11-12: *(2 rows)* Ch 1, turn, sc in each st across. (45 sc)

Row 13: Ch 2, turn, hdc in first st, hdc in each of next 44 sts. (45 hdc)

Edging & Collar: Ch 2, do not turn *(image 4)*, sc in same st as last hdc; working in sides of rows, sc in each of next 11 rows *(image 5)*; working on other side of starting chain, (sc, ch 1, hdc) in first ch *(image 6)*; hdc in next ch, 2 hdc in next ch, hdc in each of next 3 ch, 2 hdc in next ch, hdc in each of next 6 ch, 2 hdc in next ch, hdc in each of next 3 ch, 2 hdc in next st, hdc in each of next 3 ch *(image 7)*, ch 2, sl st in same st as last hdc. Leave remaining 3 ch unworked. (ch-2 corner, 13 sc, ch-1 corner, 25 hdc, ch-2 sp & 1 sl st)

Fasten off.

Side Edging: With right side facing, attach Color B to end of Row 1 *(image 8)*; working in sides of rows, sc in next row, hdc in each of next 10 rows *(image 9)*, hdc in first st on Row 13 *(at base of Jacket)*, ch 1 *(to secure last st)*. (1 sc & 11 hdc)

Fasten off and weave in all ends.

Sleeves

Note: *The Sleeves are worked around the Jacket Armholes.*

Round 1: With right side facing, working in ch-5 of Armhole, attach Color B to 3rd *(center)* ch *(image 10)*, sc in same ch, sc in each of next 2 ch; sc in side of Row 2; working in skipped sts on Row 1, sc in each of next 4 sts, sc in side of Row 2; working in ch-5, sc in each of next 2 ch. (11 sc)

Work in continuous rounds - without joining.

Round 2: Sc in each stitch around. (11 sc)

Round 3: Sc in each of next 3 sts, inc in next st, sc in each of next 5 sts, inc in next st, sc in next st. (13 sc)

Rounds 4-7: *(4 rounds)* Sc in each st around. (13 sc)

Fasten off and weave in ends.

Repeat for Second Sleeve.

Finishing Jacket - use photo as guide

1. Buttons - Using Black Floss, embroider pairs of French knots on Rows 5, 8 & 11, about 3 to 4 stitches apart.

2. Add a small snap fastener (press-stud) to the inside front of Jacket (at the end of Row 3), to secure when Jacket flap is closed. *(image 11)*

PANTS

a. *Pants are worked from top down.*

Notes for Color Changes:

b. *Change color in the last step of the previous stitch. At the end of the round, change color (if needed for beginning of next round) before joining the round.*

c. *Drop the non-working yarn to the wrong side, picking it up again for the next color change (stranding the yarn).*

Notes for Rounds 2 through 21.

d. *From Round 2, all rounds are worked in front loops only.*

e. *The rounds are joined through both loops of first stitch.*

f. *After the beginning ch-1, the first stitch is worked in the same stitch as joining.*

With Color C and smaller hook, ch 40; taking care not to twist ch, join with sl st in first ch to form a ring.

Round 1: Ch 1, working in back loops of ch-sts only, sc in each of next 4 ch; change to Color A, sc in each of next 4 ch; [change to Color C, sc in each of next 4 ch; change to Color A, sc in each of next 4 ch] 4 times; change to Color C; join with sl st to first sc. (40 sc)

See Notes for Rounds 2 through 21.

Rounds 2-3: *(2 rounds)* Ch 1, [with Color C, sc in each of next 4 sts, with Color A, sc in each of next 4 sts] 5 times; join with sl st to first sc. (40 sc)

Rounds 4-6: *(3 rounds)* Ch 1, [with Color A, sc in each of next 4 sts, with Color C, sc in each of next 4 sts] 5 times; join with sl st to first sc. (40 sc) *(image 12)*

Do not fasten off.

First Pant Leg

Round 7: Ch 1, with Color C, sc in each of next 4 sts, [with Color A, sc in each of next 4 sts, with Color C, sc in each of next 4 sts] 2 times; with Color A, ch 3 *(the 3 ch-sts between the Pants Legs)*; with Color C, ch 1 *(does not count as a stitch)*, skip next 20 sts; join with sl st to first sc. (20 sc & 3 ch-sts) *(image 13)*

Round 8: Ch 1, *(Color C)* sc in each of next 4 sts, [with Color A, sc in each of next 4 sts, with Color C, sc in each of next 4 sts] 2 times; with Color A, working in ch-3, sc in each of next 3 ch; join with sl st to first sc. (23 sc)

Round 9: Ch 1, with Color C, sc in each of next 4 sts, [with Color A, sc in each of next 4 sts, with Color C, sc in each of next 4 sts] 2 times; with Color A, sc in each of next 3 sts; join with sl st to first sc. (23 sc)

Rounds 10-12: *(3 rounds)* Ch 1, with Color A, sc in each of next 4 sts, [with Color C, sc in each of next 4 sts, with Color A, sc in each of next 4 sts] 2 times; with Color C, sc in each of next 3 sts; join with sl st to first sc. (23 sc)

Rounds 13-15: *(3 rounds)* Ch 1, with Color C, sc in each of next 4 sts, [with Color A, sc in each of next 4 sts, with Color C, sc in each of next 4 sts] 2 times; with Color A, sc in each of next 3 sts; join with sl st to first sc. (23 sc)

Rounds 16-21: Repeat Rounds 10-15 once more.

Fasten off and weave in ends.

Second Pant Leg

Starting with a long tail, attach Color C with sl st to back loop of last skipped st on Round 6. *(image 14)*

See Notes for working the Pants.

Round 7: Ch 3 *(the 3 ch-sts between the Pants Legs)*; with Color A, ch 1 *(does not count as a stitch)*, sc in first skipped st on Round 6, sc in each of next 3 sts, [with Color C, sc in each of next 4 sts, with Color A, sc in each of next 4 sts] 2 times; join with sl st to first sl st. (20 sts & 3 ch-sts)

Round 8: Ch 1, with Color C, working in ch-3, sc in each of next 3 ch, with Color A, sc in each of next 4 sts, [with Color C, sc in each of next 4 sts, with Color A, sc in each of next 4 sts] 2 times; join with sl st to first sc. (23 sc)

Round 9: Ch 1, with Color C, sc in each of next 3 sts; with Color A, sc in each of next 4 sts, [with Color C, sc in each of next 4 sts, with Color A, sc in each of next 4 sts] 2 times; join with sl st to first sc. (23 sc)

Rounds 10-12: *(3 rounds)* Ch 1, with Color A, sc in each of next 3 sts, with Color C, sc in each of next 4 sts, [with Color A, sc in each of next 4 sts, with Color C, sc in each of next 4 sts] 2 times; join with sl st to first sc. (23 sc)

Rounds 13-15: *(3 rounds)* Ch 1, with Color C, sc in each of next 3 sts, with Color A, sc in each of next 4 sts, [with Color C, sc in each of next 4 sts, with Color A, sc in each of next 4 sts] 2 times; join with sl st to first sc. (23 sc)

Rounds 16-21: Repeat Rounds 10-15 once more.

Fasten off.

1. Using long starting tail and yarn needle, close the small gap between the Legs. Weave in all ends.

Waistband

Round 1: With right side facing, working in other side of starting chain of Pants, attach Color C at center back; ch 1, sc in same ch as joining, sc in each of next 39 ch; join with sl st to first sc. (40 sc)

Round 2: Ch 1, sc in first st, sc in each of next 9 sts, dec, sc in each of next 19 sts, dec, sc in each of next 7 sts; join with sl st to first sc. (38 sc)

Fasten off and weave in ends.

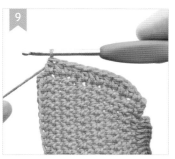
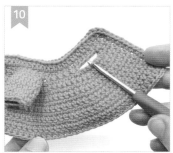

SHOE (Make 2)

Round 1: With Color C and smaller hook, ch 6, sc in 2nd ch from hook, sc in each of next 3 ch, 3 sc in last ch; working on other side of starting ch, sc in each of next 3 ch, inc in last ch. (12 sc)

Work in continuous rounds - without joining.

Round 2: Inc in next st, sc in each of next 4 sts, [inc in next st] 2 times, sc in each of next 4 sts, inc in next st. (16 sc)

Round 3: [Inc in next st] 2 times, sc in each of next 5 sts, [inc in next st] 2 times, sc in each of next 5 sts, [inc in next st] 2 times. (22 sts) *(image 15)*

Round 4: Working in back loops only, sc in each st around. (22 sc)

Round 5: Working in both loops, sc in each st around. (22 sc)

Round 6: Sc in each of next 9 sts, [dec] 3 times, sc in each of next 7 sts. (19 sc)

Round 7: Sc in each of next 9 sts, 3-dec, sc in each of next 7 sts. (17 sc)

Round 8: Sc in each st around. (17 sc)

Round 9: Sl st in each st around. (17 sl sts)

Fasten off.

Shoe Edging: With sole of Shoe facing upwards, working in unused front loops on Row 3, attach Color C to first st; sl st in each st around. (22 sl sts) *(image 16)*

Fasten off and weave in ends.

BOWL

Round 1: With Color D and smallest hook, make a magic ring; 8 sc in ring. (8 sc)

Round 2: Inc in each st around. (16 sc)

Round 3: Working in back loops only, [sc in each of next 3 sts, inc in next st] 4 times. (20 sc)

Round 4: [Sc in each of next 2 sts, inc in next st, sc in each of next 2 sts] 4 times. (24 sc)

Round 5: [Sc in each of next 5 sts, inc in next st] 4 times. (28 sc)

Round 6: [Sc in each of next 3 sts, inc in next st, sc in each of next 3 sts] 4 times. (32 sc)

Round 7: [Sc in each of next 7 sts, inc in next st] 4 times, (36 sc)

Rounds 8-10: *(3 rounds)* Sc in each st around. (36 sc)

Round 11: Sc-sp in each st around. (36 sts)

Round 12: Sl st in each st around. (36 sl sts)

Fasten off with an invisible finish and weave in ends. *(image 17)*

WOODEN SPOON

Spoon Head

Round 1: With Color E and smallest hook, make a magic ring, 8 sc in ring. (8 sc)

Finish off with an invisible join.

Handle

With Color E, make a Basic Crochet Cord, approximately 1½" (3.5 cm) in length.

Do not fasten off.

Spoon Assembly *(image 18)*

Working around Spoon Head, sc in each of next 3 sts, (hdc, dc) in next st, (dc, hdc) in next st, sc in each of next 3 sts; join with sl st in top of Handle. (10 sts) *(image 19)*

Fasten off and carefully weave in all ends. *(image 20)*

Dress Amity in her chef outfit ready for her cooking adventure!

Amity's

SNOW ADVENTURE OUTFIT

MATERIALS & TOOLS

YARN: HELLO Cotton

- **Color A:** Golden Yellow (121) for Beanie
- **Color B:** Off-White (155) for Pompom
- **Color C:** Turquoise (134) for Cowl and Mittens
- **Color D:** Lilac (139) for Ski Pants
- **Color E:** Purple (143) for Ski Pants Trim and Ski Boots

HOOK SIZE: 3.0 mm hook
2.5 mm hook for Ski Pants Trim & Ski Boots

OTHER: Pompom Maker to make a 2" (5 cm) Pompom
Embroidery Needle
⅜" (1 cm) diameter Small buttons for Ski Pants
Stitch Marker
Yarn Needle

SPECIAL STITCHES & TECHNIQUES

Bobble with 5 Double Crochet (bob)

Yarn over, insert hook in stitch or space specified and pull up a loop (3 loops on hook), yarn over and draw through two loops on hook *(2 loops remain)*, *yarn over, insert hook in same stitch or space and pull up a loop, yarn over and draw through two loops on hook; repeat from * 3 times more *(6 loops on hook)* *(image 1)*; yarn over and draw through all six loops on hook. (bobble made) *(image 2)*

Half-Double Crochet Spike Stitch (hdc-sp)

Yarn over and insert hook in specified stitch one round below current round, pull up loop to height of stitches in current round, yarn over and draw through all three loops on hook. (half-double crochet spike stitch made)

SNOW OUTFIT

BEANIE

Note: The Beanie starts with Ribbing rows, then is worked in rounds from bottom up.

Ribbing

Row 1: With Color A, ch 11, sc in 2nd ch from hook, sc in each of next 9 ch. (10 sc)

Rows 2-39: *(38 rows)* Ch 1, turn, working in back loops only, sc in each st across. (10 sc) *(image 3)*

Row 40: *(Joining Row)* Ch 1, turn, fold Ribbing so that Row 1 is behind Row 39; working through both loops of last row and the other side of the chain stitches together, matching stitches, sc in each of the 10 stiches across *(image 4)*. This joins the ends of the ribbing to form a loop. Do not fasten off.

Hat

Round 1: Ch 1, working in row ends of Ribbing, sc in each row around. (40 sc) *(image 5)*

Work in continuous rounds - without joining.

Rounds 2-6: *(5 rounds)* Sc in each st around. (40 sc)

Round 7: [Sc in each of next 4 sts, dec, sc in each of next 4 sts] 4 times. (36 sc)

Round 8: [Sc in each of next 7 sts, dec] 4 times. (32 sc)

Round 9: [Sc in each of next 3 sts, dec, sc in each of next 3 sts] 4 times. (28 sc)

Round 10: [Sc in each of next 5 sts, dec] 4 times. (24 sc)

Round 11: [Dec] 12 times. (12 sc)

Round 12: [Dec] 6 times. (6 sc)

Fasten off, leaving a long tail for sewing.

1. Use yarn needle to weave tail through the front loops of the remaining 6 stitches and pull tightly to close hole. *(image 6)*

Pompom: Using a pompom maker (or other method), make a pompom with Color B. Sew the pompom securely to top of Beanie.

COWL

With Color C, ch 34; taking care not to twist ch, join with sl st in first ch to form a ring. *(image 7)*

Round 1: Ch 1, hdc in each ch around. (34 hdc)

Work in continuous rounds - without joining.

Rounds 2-5: *(4 rounds)* Working in 3rd loops only, hdc in each st around. (34 hdc) *(images 8 & 9)*

Round 6: Working in 3rd loops only, sl st in each st around. (34 sl sts)

Fasten off and weave in ends.

MITTENS (Make 2)

Note: *Mitten thumbs are created using Bobble Stitches. Make sure the Bobbles "pop" to the right side of the work.*

Round 1: With Color C, make a magic ring, 6 sc in ring. (6 sc)

Round 2: Inc in each st around. (12 sc)

Rounds 3-4: *(2 rounds)* Sc in each st around. (12 sc)

Round 5: Sc in each of next 3 sts, bob in next st, sc in each of next 8 sts. (11 sc & 1 bobble)

Rounds 6-7: *(2 rounds)* Sc in each st around. (12 sc)

Round 8: [Sc in each of next 2 sts, inc in next st] 4 times. (16 sc) *(image 10)*

Fasten off and weave in ends.

SKI PANTS

Note: *Pants are worked from top down.*

With Color D, ch 36; taking care not to twist ch, join with sl st in first ch to form a ring.

Round 1: Ch 1, sc in each ch around; join with sl st to first sc. (36 sc)

Round 2: Ch 1, sc in first st, sc in each of next 7 sts, inc in next st, [sc in each of next 8 sts, inc in next st] 3 times; join with sl st to first sc. (40 sc)

Rounds 3-8: *(6 rounds)* Ch 1, sc in each st around; join with sl st to first sc. (40 sc) Do not fasten off.

First Pant Leg

Round 9: Ch 1, sc in first st, sc in each of next 19 sts, ch 1 *(center stitch)*, skip next 20 sts; join with sl st to first sc *(image 11)*. (20 sc & 1 ch-st)

Round 10: Ch 1, sc in first st, sc in each of next 19 sts; working in center stitch, sc in next ch. Do not join. (21 sc)

Work in continuous rounds - without joining.

Rounds 11-21: *(11 rounds)* Sc in each st around. (21 sc) Work additional sc-sts to move the end of round to the side of the Pants.

Fasten off and weave in ends.

Second Pant Leg

Starting with a long tail, attach Color D with sl st to first skipped st on Round 9. *(image 12)*

Round 9: Sc in same st as joining, sc in each of next 19 sts, ch 1 *(center stitch)*; join with sl st to first sc. (20 sc & 1 ch-st)

Round 10: Ch 1, sc in first st, sc in each of next 19 sts, working in center stitch, sc in next ch. Do not join. (21 sc)

Work in continuous rounds - without joining.

Rounds 11-21: *(11 rounds)* Sc in each st around. (21 sc) Work additional sc-sts to move the end of round to the side of the Pants.

Fasten off and weave in ends.

1. Using long starting tail and yarn needle, close the small gap between the Legs.

Waistband

Round 1: With right side facing, working in other side of starting chain of Pants, using smaller hook, attach Color E at center back *(image 13)*; ch 1, hdc in same ch as joining, hdc in each of next 13 ch, hdc-sp in next st, hdc in each of next 7 ch, hdc-sp in next st, hdc in each of next 13 ch; join with sl st to first hdc. (36 hdc) *(image 14)*

Fasten off and weave in ends.

Shoulder Straps

First Strap: With right side and front of Pants facing, using smaller hook, attach with Color E to 3rd loop of first hdc-sp on Waistband; ch 27; sc in 7th ch from hook *(button hole made)*, sc in each of next 20 ch; sl st in 3rd loop of next hdc on Waistband to secure. (21 sc & ch-6 loop)

Fasten off.

Second Strap: Repeat First Strap, starting in the other hdc-sp on Waistband.

Fasten off and weave in all ends.

Finishing Ski Pants - use photos as guide

1. Sew Buttons at back of Pants, below the Waistband, about 6 stitches apart. *(image 15)*

2. With Color E and yarn needle, embroider a snowflake on one leg of Ski Pants, using straight stitches. *(image 16)*

SKI BOOT (Make 2)

Round 1: With Color E and smaller hook, ch 6, sc in 2nd ch from hook, sc in each of next 3 ch, 3 sc in last ch; working on other side of starting ch, sc in each of next 3 ch, inc in last ch. (12 sc)

Work in continuous rounds - without joining.

Round 2: Inc in next st, sc in each of next 4 sts, [inc in next st] 2 times, sc in each of next 4 sts, inc in next st. (16 sc)

Round 3: [Inc in next st] 2 times, sc in each of next 5 sts, [inc in next st] 2 times, sc in each of next 5 sts, [inc in next st] 2 times. (22 sts) *(image 17)*

Round 4: Working in back loops only, sc in each st around. (22 sc)

Round 5: Working in both loops, sc in each st around. (22 sc)

Round 6: Sc in each of next 10 sts, dec, sc in next st, dec, sc in each of next 7 sts. (20 sc)

Round 7: Sc in each of next 8 sts, [dec] 4 times, sc in each of next 4 sts. (16 sc)

Rounds 8-9: *(2 rounds)* Sc in each st around. (16 sc)

Round 10: [Sc in each of next 3 sts, inc in next st] 4 times. (20 sc)

Round 11: Sc in each st around. (20 sc)

Fasten off.

Boot Edging: With sole of Boot facing upwards, working in unused front loops on Row 3, attach Color E to first st; sl st in each st around. (22 sl sts) *(image 18)*

Fasten off and weave in ends.

Get Amity ready for her Snow Adventure! Slide the Cowl up from the bottom, over the Legs and Body to wrap around the neck. Place the Legs in the Ski Pants and Boots. Cross the Straps at the back and fasten to the buttons. Place the Beanie on her Head.

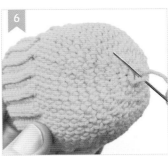

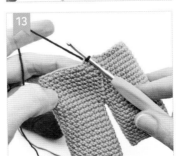

Amity's

SAFARI ADVENTURE OUTFIT

MATERIALS & TOOLS

YARN: HELLO Cotton

- **Color A:** Dark Beige (158) for Hat & Binoculars Strap
- **Color B:** Cream (156) for Trim
- **Color C:** Sage (137) for Safari Shirt
- **Color D:** Mocha (125) for Shorts
- **Color E:** Dark Brown (127) for Belt and Boots
- **Color F:** Baby Blue (146) small amount for Binoculars
- **Color G:** Black (160) for Binoculars

HOOK SIZE: 3.0 mm hook - Main hook
2.5 mm hook - for Boots
2.0 mm hook - for Binoculars

OTHER: Small amount of Stuffing for Binoculars
Stitch Marker
Yarn Needle

SPECIAL STITCHES & TECHNIQUES

Half-Double Crochet Decrease (hdc-dec)

Yarn over and insert hook in next stitch, pull up a loop (3 loops on hook), insert hook in next stitch and pull up a loop (4 loops on hook); yarn over and draw through all 4 loops. (decrease made)

SAFARI OUTFIT

HAT

Note: *Hat is worked from top down.*

With Color A, ch 40; taking care not to twist ch, join with sl st in first ch to form a ring.

Round 1: Ch 1, sc in same st as joining, sc in each of next 39 ch. (40 sc)

Work in continuous rounds - without joining.

Round 2: [Sc in each of next 9 sts, inc in next st] 4 times. (44 sc)

Round 3: [Sc in each of next 5 sts, inc in next st, sc in each of next 5 sts] 4 times. (48 sc)

Round 4: Sc in each st around. (48 sc)

Round 5: Working in back loops only, [sc in each of next 3 sts, inc in next st] 12 times. (60 sc) *(image 1)*

Round 6: [Sc in each of next 9 sts, inc in next st] 6 times. (66 sc)

Round 7: [Sc in each of next 5 sts, inc in next st, sc in each of next 5 sts] 6 times. (72 sc)

Rounds 8-9: *(2 rounds)* Sc in each st around. (72 sc)

Change to Color B.

Round 10: Sl st in each st around. (72 sl sts) *(image 2)*

Fasten off and weave in ends.

Hand Band: With Hat right-side up, using Color B, surface slip stitch between each st in Round 4 (above the unworked front loops). *(image 3)*

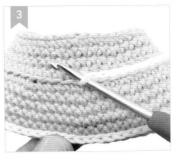

SAFARI SHIRT

Note: *Shirt is worked in rows from top down.*

Row 1: *(Right Side)* With Color C, ch 21, sc in 2nd ch from hook, sc in each of next 19 ch. (20 sc)

Row 2: Ch 1, turn, sc in first st, sc in each of next 2 sts, ch 5, skip next 4 sts *(first Armhole)*, sc in each of next 6 sts, ch 5, skip next 4 sts *(second Armhole)*, sc in each of next 3 sts. (12 sc & 2 ch-5 loops) *(image 4)*

Row 3: Ch 1, turn, sc in first st, sc in each of next 2 sts; working in ch-5, sc in each of next 5 ch; inc in next st, sc in each of next 4 sts, inc in next st; working in ch-5, sc in each of next 5 ch; sc in each of next 3 sts. (24 sc)

Row 4: Ch 1, turn, sc in first st, sc in each of next 2 sts, inc in next st, [sc in each of next 3 sts, inc in next st] 5 times. (30 sc)

Row 5: Ch 1, turn, sc in each st across. (30 sc)

Row 6: Ch 1, turn, sc in first st, sc in each of next 3 sts, inc in next st, sc in each of next 4 sts, inc in next st, sc in each of next 10 sts, [inc in next st, sc in each of next 4 sts] 2 times. (34 sc)

Rows 7-9: *(3 rows)* Ch 1, turn, sc in each st across. (34 sc)

Row 10: Ch 1, turn, sc in first st, sc in each of next 4 sts, inc in next st, sc in each of next 5 sts, inc in next st, sc in each of next 10 sts, [inc in next st, sc in each of next 5 sts] 2 times. (38 sc)

Row 11: Ch 1, turn, sc in each st across. (38 sc) *(image 5)*

Edging & Collar: Ch 1, do not turn, sc in same st as last sc made; working in sides of rows, sc in each of next 9 rows *(image 6)*; working on other side of starting ch, (sc, ch 1, 2 dc) in first ch, *(image 7)*, dc in next ch, 2 dc in next ch, dc in each of next 3 ch, 2 dc in next ch, dc in each of next 6 ch, 2 dc in next ch, dc in each of next 3 ch, 2 dc in next ch, dc in next ch, (2 dc, ch 1, sc) in last ch; working in sides of rows, sc in each of next 10 rows. (3 ch-1 corners, 22 sc & 26 dc)

Finish off with invisible join and weave in ends. *(image 8)*

Sleeves

Note: *The Sleeves are worked around the Jacket Armholes using the other side of chain-5, the 4 skipped stitches from Row 1, and working in the sides of rows on either side of the Armhole.*

Round 1: With right side facing, starting in ch-5 of Armhole, attach Color C to the ch closest to center back *(images 9 & 10)*, sc in same ch, make 10 more sc around Armhole. (11 sc)

Work in continuous rounds - without joining.

Rounds 2-5: *(4 rounds)* Sc in each st around. (11 sc)

Fasten off and weave in ends.

Repeat for Second Sleeve.

Shirt Pockets: With Color B, make 3 surface slip stitches on either side of Shirt front, between Rounds 5 & 6.

SHORTS

Note: *Shorts are worked from bottom up.*

First Leg

Round 1: With Color D, starting with a long tail, ch 17; taking care not to twist ch, join with sl st in first ch to form a ring; ch 1, sc in each ch around; join with sl st to first sc. (17 sc)

Round 2: Ch 1, sc in each st around; join with sl st to first sc. (17 sc)

Round 3: Ch 1, working in front loops only, sc in each st around. Do not join. (17 sc)

Work in continuous rounds - without joining.

Round 4: Sc in each st around. (17 sc)

Fasten off.

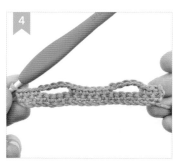
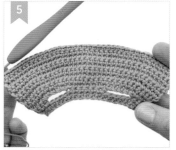

Second Leg

Rounds 1-4: *(4 rounds)* Repeat Rounds 1-4 of First Leg. Do not fasten off.

Shorts

Round 5: *(Joining Legs)* From Second leg, ch 2; working on First Leg, sc in next st *(image 11)*, sc in each of next 16 sts; working in ch-2, sc in each of next 2 ch; working on Second Leg, sc in next st, sc in each of next 16 sts; working on other side of ch-2, sc in each of next 2 ch. (38 sc) *(image 12)*

Rounds 6-10: *(5 rounds)* Sc in each st around. (38 sc)

Round 11: Sc in each of next 9 sts, dec, sc in each of next 18 sts, dec, sc in each of next 7 sts. (36 sc)

Round 12: [Sc in each of next 7 sts, dec] 4 times. (32 sc)

Fasten off and weave in end.

Cuffs: Fold up Rounds 1 & 2 of each Leg. Use starting tails and yarn needle to sew Cuffs in place. *(image 13)*

Belt: With Color E, surface slip stitch around Shorts between Rounds 11 & 12 *(image 14)*. Using yarn needle and Color D, add small vertical straight stitches as Belt Loops. *(image 15)*

Pockets: With Color B, make 4 surface slip stitches on either side of Shorts front, between Rounds 9 & 10.

BOOT (Make 2)

Round 1: With Color D and smaller hook, ch 6, sc in 2nd ch from hook, sc in each of next 3 ch, 3 sc in last ch; working on other side of starting ch, sc in each of next 3 ch, inc in last ch. (12 sc)

Work in continuous rounds - without joining.

Round 2: 2 hdc in each of next 2 sts, hdc in each of next 2 sts, 2 hdc in each of next 4 sts, hdc in each of next 2 sts, 2 hdc in each of next 2 sts. (20 hdc) *(image 16)*

Round 3: Working in both back loops and 3rd loops together, sc in each st around. (20 sc) *(image 17)*

Round 4: Sc in each st around. (20 sc)

Round 5: Sc in each of next 6 sts, [hdc-dec] 4 times, sc in each of next 6 sts. (12 sc & 4 hdc)

Round 6: Sc in each of next 6 sts, [dec] 2 times, sc in each of next 6 sts. (14 sc)

Round 7: Sc in each st around. (14 sc)

Round 8: [Inc in next st, sc in next st] 7 times. (21 sc)

Fasten off.

Boot Edging: With sole of Boot facing you, working in unused front loops on Row 2, attach Color A to first st; sl st in each st around. (20 sl sts) *(image 18)*

Fasten off and weave in ends.

BINOCULARS

Lens (Make 2)

Round 1: With Color F and smallest hook, make a magic ring, 7 sc in ring. (7 sc)

Finish off with an invisible join.

Round 2: Attach Color G to any back loop on Round 1; working in back loops only, inc in each st around. (14 sc) *(image 19)*

Work in continuous rounds - without joining.

Round 3: Working in back loops only, sc in each st around. (14 sc)

Round 4: Sc in each of next 6 sts, dec, sc in each of next 6 sts. (13 sc)

Round 5: Dec, sc in each of next 11 sts. (12 sc)

Round 6: Sc in each of next 5 sts, dec, sc in each of next 5 sts. (11 sc)

Round 7: Dec, sc in each of next 9 sts. (10 sc)

Round 8: Sc in each of next 4 sts, dec, sc in each of next 4 sts. (9 sc)

Round 9: Sc in each st around. (9 sc)

Fasten off, leaving a long tail on one Lens for sewing.

Weave in remaining ends.

1. Add a small amount of stuffing to lower half of each Lens, leaving top of Lens unstuffed and open at Round 9.

2. Using yarn needle, bring tail up through Lens, exiting between Rounds 4 & 5.

3. Position the Lenses side-by-side and secure them together with one or two stitches. *(image 20)*

Strap

With Color A and smallest hook, starting with a long tail, make a Basic Crochet Cord, about 5" (13 cm) in length.

Fasten off, leaving a long tail for sewing. *(image 21)*

1. Use yarn needle to sew tails of Strap to either side of Binoculars. *(image 22)*

Dress Amity ready for her Safari Adventure!

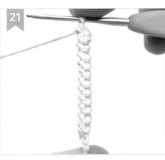

Scarlett

About 10" (25 cm) tall

MATERIALS & TOOLS

YARN: HELLO Cotton

Main color (MC): Seashell (161) for Face, Arms & Legs

Color A: Magenta (107) for Hair

Color B: Mint Green (138) for Underwear & Leaf

Color C: Cream (156) for Top & Flower

Color D: Coral (111) for Top

Color E: Sage (137) for Skirt

Color F: Salmon (109) small amount for Cheeks

HOOK SIZE: 2.5 mm hook
3.0 mm hook for Skirt

OTHER: DMC Embroidery Floss - Black for Eyes and Mouth

Embroidery Needle

Stitch Marker

Yarn Needle

Stuffing

Straight Pins

SPECIAL STITCHES & TECHNIQUES

Half Treble Crochet (htr)

Yarn over twice and insert hook in stitch or space specified, pull up a loop (4 loops on hook); yarn over, draw through 2 loops on hook, yarn over and draw through remaining 3 loops on hook. (half-treble made)

Front Post Single Crochet (FPsc)

Insert hook from front to back to front around post of indicated stitch and pull up a loop (2 loops on hook), yarn over, draw through both loops on hook.

Back Post Single Crochet (BPsc)

Insert hook from back to front to back around post of indicated stitch and pull up a loop (2 loops on hook), yarn over, draw through both loops on hook.

Front Post Half-Double Crochet (FPhdc)

Yarn over and insert hook from front to back to front around post of indicated stitch, pull up a loop (3 loops on hook), yarn over, draw through all 3 loops on hook.

Back Post Half-Double Crochet (BPhdc)

Yarn over and insert hook from back to front to back around post of indicated stitch, pull up a loop (3 loops on hook), yarn over, draw through all 3 loops on hook.

Front Post Double Crochet (FPdc)

Yarn over and insert hook from front to back to front around post of indicated stitch, pull up a loop (3 loops on hook), [yarn over, draw through 2 loops] twice.

Back Post Double Crochet (BPdc)

Yarn over and insert hook from back to front to back around post of indicated stitch, pull up a loop (3 loops on hook), [yarn over, draw through 2 loops] twice.

Unless noted otherwise, always skip the stitches behind the Post Stitches.

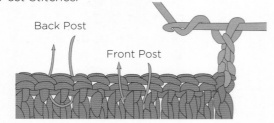

Back Post

Front Post

SCARLETT

HEAD

Front (Face)

Round 1: With MC, make a magic ring, 6 sc in ring. (6 sc)

Round 2: Inc in each st around. (12 sc)

Round 3: [Sc in next st, inc in next st] 6 times. (18 sc)

Round 4: [Sc in next st, inc in next st, sc in next st] 6 times. (24 sc)

Round 5: [Sc in each of next 3 sts, inc in next st] 6 times. (30 sc)

Round 6: [Sc in each of next 2 sts, inc in next st, sc in each of next 2 sts] 6 times. (36 sc)

Round 7: [Sc in each of next 5 sts, inc in next st] 6 times. (42 sc)

Round 8: [Sc in each of next 3 sts, inc in next st, sc in each of next 3 sts] 6 times. (48 sc)

Round 9: [Sc in each of next 7 sts, inc in next st] 6 times. (54 sc)

Round 10: [Sc in each of next 4 sts, inc in next st, sc in each of next 4 sts] 6 times. (60 sc)

Round 11: [Sc in each of next 9 sts, inc in next st] 6 times. (66 sc)

Round 12: [Sc in each of next 5 sts, inc in next st, sc in each of next 5 sts] 6 times. (72 sc)

Rounds 13-14: *(2 rounds)* Sc in each st around. (72 sc) Fasten off.

Back (Hair)

Rounds 1-13: *(13 Rounds)* With Color A, repeat Rounds 1-13 of Head Front (omitting last round). Do not fasten off. Continue with Head Assembly.

Head Assembly

1. Hold the Front and Back together with right sides facing outwards.

2. With Color A, single crochet in both the next stitch on Back and corresponding stitch on Front. This is the first stitch of the "Hairline". *(image 1)*

3. Working through both Back & Front together, single crochet in each of next 43 stitches to complete the Hairline. (44 stitches) *(image 2)*

4. Change to MC, and continue working single crochet stitches, stuffing the Head firmly before finishing the round.

5. Join the round with a slip stitch in the first single crochet stitch.

6. Fasten off and weave in ends. *(image 3)*

HAIR

Note: *Hair is worked in rows, starting with a magic ring.*

Row 1: *(Right Side)* With Color A, make a magic ring, ch 3 *(counts as first dc, now and throughout)*, 5 dc in ring. (6 dc) Tighten ring but do not join round.

Row 2: Ch 3, turn, dc in first st, 2 dc in each of next 4 sts, 2 dc in last st *(3rd ch of ch-3)*. (12 dc)

Row 3: Ch 3, turn, dc in first st, [dc in next st, 2 dc in next st] 5 times, dc in last st. (18 dc)

Row 4: Ch 3, turn, [2 dc in first st, dc in each of next 2 sts] 5 times, 2 dc in next st, dc in last st. (24 dc)

Row 5: Ch 3, turn, dc in first st, dc in each of next 23 sts. (25 dc)

Row 6: Ch 4 *(counts as first tr, now and throughout)*, turn, tr in first st, tr in each of next 3 sts, dc in each of next 16 sts, tr in each of next 4 sts, tr in last st. (10 tr & 16 dc) *(image 4)*

Row 7: Ch 4, turn, tr in first st, tr in each of next 2 sts, 2 htr in next st, hdc in next st, sl st in each of next 2 sts, [ch 4, tr is same st, tr in each of next 2 sts, 2 htr in next st, hdc in next st, sl st in each of next 2 sts] 2 times, sl st in next st, hdc in next st, 2 htr in next st, tr in each of next 4 sts. (16 tr, 8 htr, 4 hdc & 5 sl sts) *(images 5 & 6)*

Fasten off, leaving a long tail for sewing.

1. Position the Hair on Head Front, gently shaping to fit full length of Hairline, and securing with pins. *(image 7)*

2. Using the long tail and yarn needle, sew the Hair in place along the Hairline. *(images 8 & 9)*

Hair Side Piece - A (Make 2)

Row 1: *(Wrong Side)* With Color A, ch 7, sc in 2nd ch from hook, sc in each of next 5 ch. (6 sc)

Row 2: *(Right Side)* Ch 4, turn, tr in first st, tr in each of next 2 sts, 2 htr in next st, hdc in next st, sl st in last st. (4 tr, 2 htr, 1 hdc)

Fasten off, leaving a long tail for sewing.

Hair Side Piece - B (Make 2)

Row 1: *(Wrong Side)* With Color A, ch 7, sc in 2nd ch from hook, sc in each of next 5 ch. (6 sc)

Row 2: *(Right Side)* Ch 1, turn, skip first st, hdc in next st, 2 htr in next st, tr in each of next 3 sts, ch 4, sl st in same st as last tr. (1 hdc, 2 htr, & 4 tr)

Fasten off.

Assembly of Hair Side Pieces

1. Hold an A and B piece together, matching the shaping, and right sides facing outwards. *(image 10)*

2. Using the long tail and yarn needle, sew the pieces together across the top of Row 2 and then down the ch-4. Do not fasten off.

3. Repeat steps 1 & 2 for remaining A and B pieces.

4. Position the joined Side Pieces (with the ch-4 to the top) on either side of the Head, just below the end of the Hairline. *(image 11)*

5. Using same long tail, sew Side Pieces (across the starting chains) securely to the last round at back of Head. *(images 12 & 13)*

6. Weave in all ends and set Head aside. *(image 14)*

ARM (Make 2)

Round 1: With MC, make a magic ring, 6 sc in ring. (6 sc)

Round 2: Inc in each st around. (12 sc)

Rounds 3-5: *(3 rounds)* Sc in each st around. (12 sc)

Round 6: [Dec, sc in each of next 4 sts] 2 times. (10 sc)

Rounds 7-21: *(15 rounds)* Sc in each st around. (10 sc)

Fasten off.

1. Stuff the Hands, leaving the remainder of Arm unstuffed.

2. Set Arms aside.

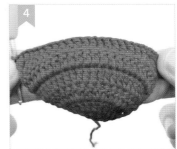

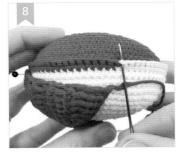

LEGS & BODY

First Leg

Round 1: With MC, make a magic ring, 6 sc in ring. (6 sc)

Round 2: Inc in each st around. (12 sc)

Rounds 3-24: *(22 rounds)* Sc in each st around. (12 sc)

Round 25: [Inc in next st, sc in each of next 5 sts] 2 times. (14 sc)

Rounds 26-28: *(3 rounds)* Sc in each st around. (14 sc)

Round 29: Sc in next st, inc in next st, sc in each of next 6 sts, inc in next st, sc in each of next 5 sts. (16 sc)

Round 30: Sc in each st around. (16 sc) Sc in each of next 2 sts *(to move the end of round to the side of Leg)*.

Fasten off.

Second Leg

Rounds 1-30: *(30 rounds)* With MC, repeat Rounds 1-30 of First Leg (including extra 2 sc).

Change to Color B. Do not fasten off.

Stuff both Legs firmly. Continue with Body.

Body

Round 1: *(Joining Legs)* From Second Leg *(Color B)*, ch 2; working on First Leg, sc in next st *(image 15)*, sc in each of next 15 sts; working in ch-2, sc in each of next 2 ch; working on Second Leg, sc in each of next 16 sts; working on other side of ch-2, sc in each of next 2 ch. (36 sc)

Round 2: [Sc in each of next 5 sts, inc in next st] 6 times. (42 sc) *(image 16)*

Rounds 3-8: *(6 rounds)* Sc in each st around. (42 sc)

Change to Color C. Cut Color B.

Continue in a stripe pattern, alternating Color C and Color D each round.

Round 9: *(Color C)* Working in back loops only, sc in each of next 9 sts, dec, sc in each of next 20 sts, dec, sc in each of next 9 sts. (40 sc)

Round 10: *(Color D)* Sc in each st around. (40 sc)

Start stuffing Body.

Round 11: *(Color C)* Sc in each of next 10 sts, dec, sc in each of next 18 sts, dec, sc in each of next 8 sts. (38 sc)

Round 12: *(Color D)* Sc in each st around. (38 sc)

Round 13: *(Color C)* Sc in each of next 9 sts, dec, sc in each of next 18 sts, dec, sc in each of next 7 sts. (36 sc)

Round 14: *(Color D)* Sc in each st around. (36 sc)

Round 15: *(Color C)* [Sc in each of next 7 sts, dec] 4 times. (32 sc)

Round 16: *(Color D)* Sc in each of next 9 sts, dec, sc in each of next 14 sts, dec, sc in each of next 5 sts. (30 sc)

Rounds 17: *(Color C)* Sc in each st around. (30 sc)

Round 18: *(Color D)* Sc in each of next 8 sts, dec, sc in each of next 14 sts, dec, sc in each of next 4 sts. (28 sc)

Round 19: *(Color C)* Sc in each of next 8 sts, dec, sc in each of next 13 sts, dec, sc in each of next 3 sts. (26 sc)

Round 20: *(Color D)* Sc in each of next 8 sts, dec, sc in each of next 12 sts, dec, sc in each of next 2 sts. (24 sc)

Note: *When attaching each Arm, flatten the top of the Arm and hold against the Body. Work the "attaching" stitches through both the layers of the Arm and the Body together.*

Round 21: *(Attaching Arms – Color C)* Sc in each of next 6 sts; working on First Arm & Body, sc in each of next 5 sts *(First Arm attached) (image 17 & 18)*; working on Body only, sc in each of next 8 sts; working on Second Arm & Body, sc in each of next 5 sts *(Second Arm attached)*. (24 sc)

Round 22: *(Color D)* [Sc in each of next 2 sts, dec] 6 times. (18 sc)

Round 23: *(Color C)* [Sc in each of next 7 sts, dec] 2 times. (16 sc)

Change to MC.

Rounds 24: *(Neck)* Sc in each st around. (16 sc)

Fasten off, leaving a long tail for sewing.

1. Finish stuffing the Body.

SKIRT

Note for Round 7: *Work the single crochet in the next stitch, then work the Front Post stitch around the same stitch.*

With Legs pointing up, using larger hook, attach Color E to first unworked front loop on Round 8 of Body.

Round 1: Working in unworked front loops only *(image 19)*, sc in each st around. (42 sc)

Work in continuous rounds – without joining.

Round 2: [Sc in each of next 3 sts, inc in next st, sc in each of next 3 sts] 6 times. (48 sc)

Round 3: [Sc in each of next 7 sts, inc in next st] 6 times. (54 sc)

Round 4: [FPsc in next st, BPsc in next st] around. (54 sts) *(image 20)*

Rounds 5-6: *(2 rounds)* [FPhdc in next st, BPhdc in next st] around. (54 sts)

Round 7: [(Sc, FPdc) in next st, BPdc in next st] around. (81 sts) *(image 21)*

Fasten off and weave in ends. *(image 22)*

FINISHING THE DOLL – use photos as guide

1. Using long tail and yarn needle, sew Body to Head, working through all 16 sts around Neck. *(images 23 & 24)*

TIP: *Ensure Body is centered between Hair Side Pieces. Maintain a wide, round Neck opening, adding extra stuffing before finishing.*

Face (image 25)

TIP: *Use straight pins to mark positions of facial features, based on preferred placement.*

1. With Black Floss (using 4 to 6 strands, depending on preferred thickness), embroider Mouth over Round 10 on Face. With Color D, embroider small straight stitch in center of Mouth.

2. For Eyes, embroider several vertical straight stitches (over 2 stitches each).

3. Use 2 strands of Floss and embroider Eyelashes and Eyebrows.

4. With Color F and yarn needle, embroider a few short, straight stitches under the outer edge of each Eye, to add Cheek markings.

Flower Pin

Leaf: With Color B, make a magic ring, ch 2, dc in ring, ch 1, sc under both front loop and side of dc just made *(image 26)*, (dc, hdc, sl st) in ring. Tighten ring. *(image 27)*

Fasten off, leaving a long tail for sewing.

Flower: With Color C, ch 22; 2 hdc in 3rd from hook, 2 hdc in each of next 19 ch. (40 hdc).

Fasten off, leaving a long tail for sewing.

1. Coil the Flower into shape. *(image 28)*

2. Use long tail and yarn needle to secure the shape.

3. Attach the Leaf to back of Flower before sewing to front of Body. *(image 29)*

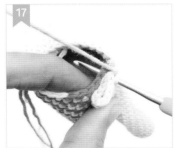

Marigold

About 10" (25 cm) tall

MATERIALS & TOOLS

YARN: HELLO Cotton

Main color (MC): Misty Rose (163) for Face, Arms & Legs

Color A: Lilac (139) for Hair

Color B: Dark Purple (144) for Pants

Color C: Dark Yellow (120) for Dress

Color D: Golden Yellow (121) for Dress

Color E: Orange (119) for Dress

Color F: Bright Orange (118) for Dress & Flower

Color G: Salmon (109) small amount for Cheeks

HOOK SIZE: 2.5 mm hook

OTHER: DMC Embroidery Floss - Black for Eyes and Mouth

Embroidery Needle

Stitch Marker

Yarn Needle

Stuffing

Straight Pins

SPECIAL STITCHES & TECHNIQUES

Double Crochet Decrease (dc-dec)

Yarn over and insert hook in stitch or space specified, pull up a loop (3 loops on hook), yarn over and draw through two loops on hook (2 loops remain on hook); yarn over, insert hook in next stitch or space and pull up a loop (4 loops on hook), yarn over and draw through two loops on hook (3 loops remain on hook). Yarn over and draw through all three loops on hook. (double crochet decrease made)

MARIGOLD

HEAD

Front (Face)

Round 1: With MC, make a magic ring, 6 sc in ring. (6 sc)

Round 2: Inc in each st around. (12 sc)

Round 3: [Sc in next st, inc in next st] 6 times. (18 sc)

Round 4: [Sc in next st, inc in next st, sc in next st] 6 times. (24 sc)

Round 5: [Sc in each of next 3 sts, inc in next st] 6 times. (30 sc)

Round 6: [Sc in each of next 2 sts, inc in next st, sc in each of next 2 sts] 6 times. (36 sc)

Round 7: [Sc in each of next 5 sts, inc in next st] 6 times. (42 sc)

Round 8: [Sc in each of next 3 sts, inc in next st, sc in each of next 3 sts] 6 times. (48 sc)

Round 9: [Sc in each of next 7 sts, inc in next st] 6 times. (54 sc)

Round 10: [Sc in each of next 4 sts, inc in next st, sc in each of next 4 sts] 6 times. (60 sc)

Round 11: [Sc in each of next 9 sts, inc in next st] 6 times. (66 sc)

Round 12: [Sc in each of next 5 sts, inc in next st, sc in each of next 5 sts] 6 times. (72 sc)

Rounds 13-14: *(2 rounds)* Sc in each st around. (72 sc) Fasten off.

Back (Hair)

Rounds 1-13: *(13 Rounds)* With Color A, repeat Rounds 1-13 of Head Front (omitting last round). Do not fasten off. Continue with Head Assembly.

Head Assembly

1. Hold the Front and Back together with right sides facing outwards. *(image 1)*

2. With Color A, single crochet in both the next stitch on Back and corresponding stitch on Front. This is the first stitch of the "Hairline". *(image 2)*

3. Working through both Back & Front together, single crochet in each of next 49 stitches to complete the Hairline. (50 stitches) *(image 3)*

4. Change to MC, and continue working single crochet

stitches, stuffing the Head firmly before finishing the round. *(image 4)*

5. Join the round with a slip stitch in the first single crochet stitch.

6. Fasten off and weave in ends.

HAIR

Note: *Hair is worked in rows, starting with a magic ring.*

Row 1: *(Right Side)* With Color A, make a magic ring, ch 3 *(counts as first dc, now and throughout)*, 5 dc in ring. (6 dc) Tighten ring but do not join round.

Row 2: Ch 3, turn, dc in first st, 2 dc in each of next 4 sts, 2 dc in last st *(3rd ch of ch-3)*. (12 dc)

Row 3: Ch 3, turn, dc in first st, [dc in next st, 2 dc in next st] 5 times, dc in last st. (18 dc)

Row 4: Ch 3, turn, dc in first st, [dc in each of next 2 sts, 2 dc in first st] 5 times, dc in each of next 2 sts. (24 dc)

Row 5: Ch 3, turn, dc in first st, dc in each of next 23 sts. (25 dc)

First Side

Row 6a: Ch 3, turn, dc in first st, dc in each of next 12 sts, dc-dec. (15 dc) Leave remaining sts unworked. *(image 5)*

Row 7a: Ch 2 *(counts as a st, now and throughout)*, turn, dc-dec *(using next 2 sts)*, dc in each of next 11 sts. (13 sts) Leave remaining st *(ch-3)* unworked.

Row 8a: Ch 3, turn, dc in each of next 7 sts, dc-dec. (9 dc) Leave remaining sts unworked.

Row 9a: Ch 2, turn, dc-dec *(using next 2 sts)*, dc in each of next 5 sts, dc in last st *(3rd ch of ch-3)* (8 sts)

Row 10a: Ch 3, turn, dc in each of next 2 sts, dc-dec. (4 dc) Leave remaining sts unworked.

Row 11a: Ch 2, turn, dc-dec *(using next 2 sts)*. (2 sts) Leave remaining st *(ch-3)* unworked.

Fasten off, leaving a long tail for sewing.

Second Side

Row 6b: With right side facing, attach Color A to first st on Row 5 *(3rd ch of ch-3)*, ch 3 *(image 6)*, dc in each of next 4 sts, dc-dec. (6 dc) Leave remaining sts unworked.

Row 7b: Ch 2, turn, dc-dec *(using next 2 sts)*, dc in each of next 2 sts. (4 sts) Leave remaining st *(ch-3)* unworked.

Row 8b: Ch 3, turn, dc-dec. (2 dc)

Fasten off. *(image 7)*

1. Position the Hair on Head Front, gently shaping to fit full length of Hairline, and securing with pins. *(image 8)*

2. Using the long tail and yarn needle, sew the Hair in place along the Hairline. *(images 9 & 10)*

Side Bun

Row 1: With Color A, ch 6, 3 tr in 4th ch from hook, 3 dc in next ch, (3 tr, ch 2, sl st) in last ch. (9 sts & 1 ch-2)

Fasten off, leaving a long tail for sewing.

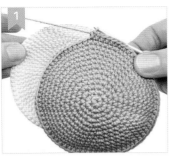

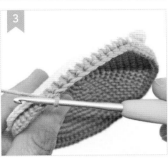
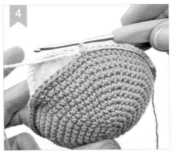
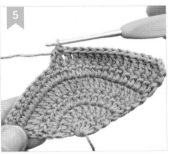

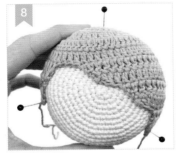

1. Flatten Bun and position below Row 8b of Hair, just behind the Hairline. *(image 11)*

2. Using long tail and yarn needle, sew in place.

3. Set Head aside.

ARM (Make 2)

Round 1: With MC, make a magic ring, 6 sc in ring. (6 sc)

Round 2: Inc in each st around. (12 sc)

Rounds 3-5: *(3 rounds)* Sc in each st around. (12 sc)

Round 6: [Dec, sc in each of next 4 sts] 2 times. (10 sc)

Rounds 7-21: *(15 rounds)* Sc in each st around. (10 sc)

Round 22: [Dec, sc in each of next 3 sts] 2 times. (8 sc) Fasten off.

1. Stuff the Hands, leaving the remainder of Arm unstuffed.

2. Set Arms aside.

LEGS & BODY

First Leg

Round 1: With Color MC, make a magic ring, 6 sc in ring. (6 sc)

Round 2: Inc in each st around. (12 sc)

Rounds 3-12: *(10 rounds)* Sc in each st around. (12 sc) Change to Color B.

Rounds 13-15: *(3 rounds)* Sc in each st around. (12 sc)

Round 16: Inc in next st, sc in each of next 11 sts. (13 sc)

Rounds 17-19: *(3 rounds)* Sc in each st around. (13 sc)

Round 20: Inc in next st, sc in each of next 12 sts. (14 sc)

Rounds 21-23: *(3 rounds)* Sc in each st around. (14 sc)

Round 24: Inc in next st, sc in each of next 13 sts. (15 sc)

Rounds 25-27: *(3 rounds)* Sc in each st around. (15 sc)

Round 28: Inc in next st, sc in each of next 14 sts. (16 sc)

Rounds 29-31: *(3 rounds)* Sc in each st around. (16 sc) Fasten off.

Second Leg

Rounds 1-31: *(31 rounds)* Repeat Rounds 1-31 of First Leg. (16 sc). Sc in each of next 8 sts *(to move the end of round to the side of Leg)*. Do not fasten off.

Stuff both Legs firmly. Continue with Body.

Body

Round 1: *(Joining Legs)* From Second Leg, ch 2; working on First Leg, sc in next st *(image 12)*, sc in each of next 15 sts; working in ch-2, sc in each of next 2 ch; working on Second Leg, sc in each of next 16 sts; working on other side of ch-2, sc in each of next 2 ch. (36 sc)

Round 2: [Sc in each of next 5 sts, inc in next st] 6 times. (42 sc)

Rounds 3-8: *(6 rounds)* Sc in each st around. (42 sc)

Round 9: Sc in each of next 9 sts, dec, sc in each of next 20 sts, dec, sc in each of next 9 sts. (40 sc)

Round 10: Sc in each st around. (40 sc)

Change to Color MC. Start stuffing Body.

Round 11: Sc in each of next 9 sts, dec, sc in each of next 19 sts, dec, sc in each of next 8 sts. (38 sc)

Round 12: Sc in each st around. (38 sc)

Round 13: Sc in each of next 9 sts, dec, sc in each of next 18 sts, dec, sc in each of next 7 sts. (36 sc)

Round 14: Sc in each st around. (36 sc)

Round 15: [Sc in each of next 7 sts, dec] 4 times. (32 sc)

Round 16: Sc in each of next 9 sts, dec, sc in each of next 14 sts, dec, sc in each of next 5 sts. (30 sc)

Round 17: Sc in each st around. (30 sc)

Round 18: Sc in each of next 9 sts, dec, sc in each of next 13 sts, dec, sc in each of next 4 sts. (28 sc)

Round 19: [Sc in each of next 5 sts, dec] 4 times. (24 sc)

Round 20: Sc in each of next 8 sts, dec, sc in each of next 10 sts, dec, sc in each of next 2 sts. (22 sc)

Note: *When attaching each Arm, flatten the top of the Arm and hold against the Body. Work the "attaching" stitches through both the layers of the Arm and the Body together.*

Round 21: *(Attaching Arms)* Sc in each of next 7 sts; working on First Arm & Body, sc in each of next 4 sts *(First Arm attached)*; working on Body only, sc in each of next 7 sts; working on Second Arm & Body, sc in each of next 4 sts *(Second Arm attached)*. (22 sc) *(images 13 & 14)*

Round 22: Sc in each of next 7 sts, [dec] 2 times, sc in each of next 7 sts, [dec] 2 times. (18 sc)

Round 23: [Sc in each of next 7 sts, dec] 2 times. (16 sc)

Rounds 24-25: *(Neck - 2 rounds)* Sc in each st around. (16 sc) *(image 15)*

Fasten off, leaving a long tail for sewing.

1. Finish stuffing the Body.

2. Set Body aside.

DRESS

Note: *Dress is worked from top down in joined rounds.*

With Color C, ch 24; taking care not to twist ch, join with sl st in first ch to form a ring.

Round 1: Ch 1, sc in same ch as joining, sc in each of next 2 ch, 3 sc in next ch *(corner)*, sc in each of next 4 ch, 3 sc in next ch *(corner)*, sc in each of next 6 ch, 3 sc in next ch *(corner)*, sc in each of next 4 ch, 3 sc in next ch *(corner)*, sc in each of next 3 ch. (32 sc)

Work in continuous rounds - without joining.

Note: *The 3-sc corners are worked in the center sc of the 3-sc corners on the previous round.*

Round 2: Sc in each of next 4 sts, 3 sc in next st, sc in each of next 6 sts, 3 sc in next st, sc in each of next 8 sts, 3 sc in next st, sc in each of next 6 sts, 3 sc in next st, sc

in each of next 4 sts. (40 sc)

Round 3: Sc in each of next 5 sts, 3 sc in next st, sc in each of next 8 sts, 3 sc in next st, sc in each of next 10 sts, 3 sc in next st, sc in each of next 8 sts, 3 sc in next st, sc in each of next 5 sts. (48 sc)

Round 4: Sc in each of next 6 sts, 3 sc in next st, sc in each of next 10 sts, 3 sc in next st, sc in each of next 12 sts, 3 sc in next st, sc in each of next 10 sts, 3 sc in next st, sc in each of next 6 sts. (56 sc)

Round 5: Sc in each of next 7 sts, 3 sc in next st, sc in each of next 12 sts, 3 sc in next st, sc in each of next 14 sts, 3 sc in next st, sc in each of next 12 sts, 3 sc in next st, sc in each of next 7 sts. (64 sc) *(image 16)*

Round 6: Sc in each of next 8 sts, 3 sc in next st, sc in each of next 14 sts, 3 sc in next st, sc in each of next 16 sts, 3 sc in next st, sc in each of next 14 sts, 3 sc in next st, sc in each of next 8 sts. (72 sc)

Note: *For the Armholes, work to the center sc of 3-sc corner, skip the stitches and start working in the center sc of next 3-sc corner.*

Round 7: Sc in each of next 10 sts, skip next 16 sts *(first Armhole)*, sc in each of next 20 sts, skip 16 sts *(second Armhole)*, sc in each of next 10 sts. (40 sc) *(image 17)*

Round 8: Sc in each st around. (40 sc)

Change to Color B.

Round 9: Working in back loops only, hdc in each st around. (40 hdc) *(image 18)*

Change to Color D.

Round 10: [Sc in each of next 4 sts, inc in next st] 8 times. (48 sc)

Round 11: Sc in each st around. (48 sc)

Round 12: Sc in each of next 2 sts, ch 3, skip next 3 sts, [sc in each of next 3 sts, ch 3, skip next 3 sts] 7 times, sc in next st. (24 sc & 8 ch-3 loops) *(image 19)*

Round 13: [Sc in next st, skip next st, 7 dc in ch-3 loop, skip next st] 8 times. (8 sc & 8 dc-7 shells) *(image 20)* Sc in each of next 4 sts *(to move end of round to 3rd dc of first shell)*.

Round 14: Sc in each of next 2 sts, [ch 3, skip next 5 sts, sc in each of next 3 sts] 7 times, ch 3, skip next 5 sts, sc in next st. (24 sc & 8 ch-3 loops) *(image 21)*

Change to Color E.

Round 15: [Sc in next st, skip next st, 7 dc in ch-3 loop, skip next st] 8 times. *(image 22)* (8 sc & 8 dc-7 shells) Sc in each of next 4 sts *(to move end of round to 3rd dc of first shell)*.

Round 16: Sc in each of next 2 sts, [ch 3, skip next 5 sts, sc in each of next 3 sts] 7 times, ch 3, skip next 5 sts, sc in next st. (24 sc & 8 ch-3 loops)

Change to Color F.

Round 17: [Sc in next st, skip next st, 7 dc in ch-3 loop, skip next st] 8 times. *(image 23)* (8 sc & 8 dc-7 shells) Sl st in next st. Fasten off and weave in ends.

FINISHING THE DOLL - use photos as guide

1. Place the Dress on Body. *(image 24)*

2. Using long tail and yarn needle, sew Body to Head, working through all 16 sts around Neck. *(image 25)*

TIP: Ensure Body is centered between the Hair Bun and end of Hairline on other side of Head. Maintain a wide, round Neck opening, adding extra stuffing before finishing.

Face

TIP: Use straight pins to mark positions of facial features, based on preferred placement.

1. With Black Floss (using 4 to 6 strands, depending on preferred thickness), embroider Mouth over Round 10 on Face.

2. For Eyes, create arcs about 3-4 rounds wide and 2-3 stitches tall.

3. Use 2 strands of Floss and embroider Eyebrows above the Eyes.

4. With Color G and yarn needle, embroider a few short, straight stitches under the outer edge of each Eye, to add Cheek markings. *(image 26)*

Flower

Round 1: With Color F, make a magic ring, 6 sc in ring. (6 sc)

Round 2: [Sl st in back loop of next st, ch 2, 2 dc in same back loop, ch 2, sl st in back loop of next st] 4 times; sl st in back loop of each of next 2 sts. (4 "petals" & 2 sl sts)

Round 3: Sl st in each of next 2 unworked front loops from Round 1, [ch 1, dc in same front loop, ch 1, sl st in front loop of next st on Round 1] 2 times, ch 1, (dc, ch 1, sl st) in same front loop. (3 "petals") Leave remaining sts unworked. *(image 27)*

Fasten off, leaving a long tail for sewing.

1. Use long tail and yarn needle to sew Flower to side of Hair, just above Bun, using pictures as a guide. *(image 28)*

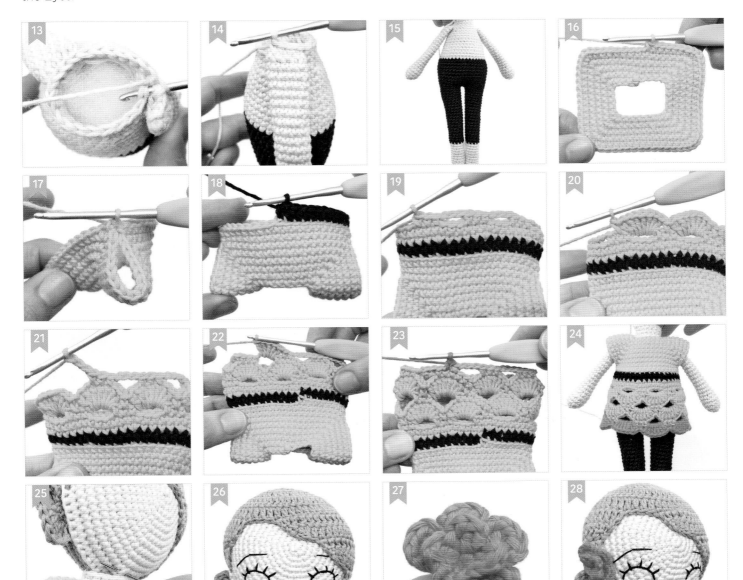

Freya

About 10" (25 cm) tall

MATERIALS & TOOLS

YARN: HELLO Cotton

- **Main color (MC):** Misty Rose (163) for Face, Arms & Legs
- **Color A:** Dark Salmon (112) for Hair
- **Color B:** Off-white (155) for Top
- **Color C:** Grey Blue (149) for Tights & Hair Clip
- **Color D:** Dusty Blue (145) for Dress
- **Color E:** Apricot (110) for Pockets
- **Color F:** Coral (111) small amount for Cheeks

OTHER: 2.5 mm hook
3.0 mm hook for Dress (lower half only)

OTHER: DMC Embroidery Floss - Black
for Eyes and Mouth
Embroidery Needle
Stitch Marker
Yarn Needle
Stuffing
Straight Pins

SPECIAL STITCHES & TECHNIQUES

Double Crochet Decrease (dc-dec)
Yarn over and insert hook in stitch or space specified, pull up a loop (3 loops on hook), yarn over and draw through two loops on hook (2 loops remain on hook); yarn over, insert hook in next stitch or space and pull up a loop (4 loops on hook), yarn over and draw through two loops on hook (3 loops remain on hook). Yarn over and draw through all three loops on hook. (double crochet decrease made)

Half Treble Crochet (htr)
Yarn over twice and insert hook in stitch or space specified, pull up a loop (4 loops on hook); yarn over, draw through 2 loops on hook, yarn over and draw through remaining 3 loops on hook. (half-treble made)

FREYA

HEAD

Front (Face)
Round 1: With MC, make a magic ring, 6 sc in ring. (6 sc)

Round 2: Inc in each st around. (12 sc)

Round 3: [Sc in next st, inc in next st] 6 times. (18 sc)

Round 4: [Sc in next st, inc in next st, sc in next st] 6 times. (24 sc)

Round 5: [Sc in each of next 3 sts, inc in next st] 6 times. (30 sc)

Round 6: [Sc in each of next 2 sts, inc in next st, sc in each of next 2 sts] 6 times. (36 sc)

Round 7: [Sc in each of next 5 sts, inc in next st] 6 times. (42 sc)

Round 8: [Sc in each of next 3 sts, inc in next st, sc in each of next 3 sts] 6 times. (48 sc)

Round 9: [Sc in each of next 7 sts, inc in next st] 6 times. (54 sc)

Round 10: [Sc in each of next 4 sts, inc in next st, sc in each of next 4 sts] 6 times. (60 sc)

Round 11: [Sc in each of next 9 sts, inc in next st] 6 times. (66 sc)

Round 12: [Sc in each of next 5 sts, inc in next st, sc in each of next 5 sts] 6 times. (72 sc)

Rounds 13-14: (2 rounds) Sc in each st around. (72 sc)
Fasten off.

Back (Hair)
Rounds 1-13: (13 Rounds) With Color A, repeat Rounds 1-13 of Head Front (omitting last round). Do not fasten off. Continue with Head Assembly.

Head Assembly
1. Hold the Front and Back together with right sides facing outwards.

2. With Color A, single crochet in both the next stitch on Back and corresponding stitch on Front. (image 1) This is the first stitch of the "Hairline".

3. Working through both Back & Front together, single crochet in each of next 53 stitches to complete the Hairline. (54 stitches) (image 2)

4. Change to MC, and continue working single crochet stitches, stuffing the Head firmly before finishing the round. (image 3)

5. Join the round with a slip stitch in the first single crochet stitch.

6. Fasten off and weave in ends. (image 4)

HAIR

Note: Hair is worked in rows, starting with a magic ring.

Row 1: (Wrong Side) With Color A, make a magic ring, ch 3 (counts as first dc, now and throughout), 5 dc in ring. (6 dc) Tighten ring but do not join round.

Row 2: (Right Side) Ch 3, turn, dc in first st, 2 dc in each of next 4 sts, 2 dc in last st (3rd ch of ch-3). (12 dc)

Row 3: Ch 3, turn, dc in first st, [dc in next st, 2 dc in next st] 5 times, dc in last st. (18 dc)

Row 4: Ch 3, turn, [2 dc in next st, dc in each of next 2 sts] 5 times, 2 dc in next st, dc in last st. (24 dc)

Row 5: Ch 3, turn, dc in each of next 23 sts. (24 dc)

Row 6: Ch 1, turn, hdc in first st, dc in next st, [htr in each of next 3 sts, 2 htr in next st] 3 times, htr in each of next 9 sts, htr in last st. (27 sts)

Row 7: Ch 3, turn, dc in each of next 6 sts, dc-dec (using next 2 sts) (8 dc) Leave remaining sts unworked.

Row 8: Ch 2 (counts as first st, now and throughout), turn, dc in each of next 7 sts. (8 sts)

Row 9: Ch 3, turn, dc in each of next 5 sts, dc-dec (using next st & 2nd ch of ch-2). (7 dc)

Row 10: Ch 2, turn, dc in each of next 5 sts. (6 sts) Leave remaining st (ch-3) unworked.

Row 11: Ch 3, turn, dc in each next 3 sts, dc-dec (using next st & 2nd ch of ch-2). (5 dc)

Row 12: Ch 1, skip first st, sc in next st, hdc in next st, dc in next st. (3 sts) Leave remaining st (ch-3) unworked.

Fasten off, leaving a long tail for sewing. (image 5)

1. Position the Hair on Head Front, gently shaping to fit full length of Hairline, and securing with pins. (image 6)

2. Using the long tail and yarn needle, sew the Hair in place along the Hairline. (images 7 & 8)

Hair Bun (Make 4)

Note: Bun is worked in rows, starting with a magic ring. The beginning ch-3 does NOT count as a stitch.

Row 1: (Wrong Side) With Color A, make a magic ring, ch 3, 8 dc in ring. (8 dc) Tighten ring but do not join round.

Row 2: *(Right Side)* Ch 3, turn, dc in first, 2 dc in each of next 7 sts. (15 dc)

Fasten off, leaving a long tail on 2 of the Hair Buns.

1. Hold two Hair Buns (one with a long tail) together with right sides facing outwards.

2. Using long tail and yarn needle, whip stitch across tops of Row 2 to join pieces together. *(image 9)*

3. Repeat with remaining two Hair Buns. *(image 10)*

4. Position the Buns on either side of Head, just behind Hairline, with center of Bun aligned with end of Hairline. *(image 11)*

5. Using same long tails, sew Buns in place. *(images 12 & 13)*

6. Set Head aside.

ARM (Make 2)

Round 1: With MC, make a magic ring, 6 sc in ring. (6 sc)

Round 2: Inc in each st around. (12 sc)

Rounds 3-5: *(3 rounds)* Sc in each st around. (12 sc)

Round 6: [Dec, sc in each of next 4 sts] 2 times. (10 sc)

Change to Color B.

Rounds 7-21: *(15 rounds)* Sc in each st around. (10 sc) *(image 14)* Fasten off.

1. Stuff the lower third of each Arm, leaving the remainder of Arm unstuffed.

2. Set Arms aside.

LEGS & BODY

First Leg

Round 1: With Color C, make a magic ring, 6 sc in ring. (6 sc)

Round 2: Inc in each st around. (12 sc)

Rounds 3-24: *(22 rounds)* Sc in each st around. (12 sc)

Round 25: [Inc in next st, sc in each of next 5 sts] 2 times. (14 sc)

Rounds 26-28: *(3 rounds)* Sc in each st around. (14 sc)

Round 29: Sc in next st, inc in next st, sc in each of next 6 sts, inc in next st, sc in each of next 5 sts. (16 sc)

Round 30: Sc in each st around. (16 sc) Sc in each of next 2 sts *(to move the end of round to the side of Leg)*.

Fasten off.

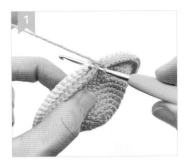
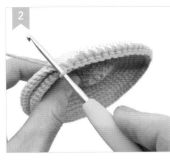

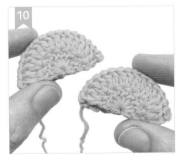

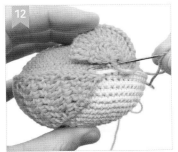

Second Leg

Rounds 1-30: *(30 rounds)* With Color C, repeat Rounds 1-30 of First Leg (including extra 2 sc). Do not fasten off.

Stuff both Legs firmly. Continue with Body.

Body

Round 1: *(Joining Legs)* From Second Leg, ch 2; working on First Leg, sc in next st, sc in each of next 15 sts; working in ch-2, sc in each of next 2 ch; working on Second Leg, sc in each of next 16 sts; working on other side of ch-2, sc in each of next 2 ch. (36 sc)

Round 2: [Sc in each of next 5 sts, inc in next st] 6 times. (42 sc) *(image 15)*

Rounds 3-8: *(6 rounds)* Sc in each st around. (42 sc)

Round 9: Sc in each of next 10 sts, dec, sc in each of next 19 sts, dec, sc in each of next 9 sts. (40 sc)

Round 10: Sc in each st around. (40 sc)

Change to Color B.

Start stuffing Body.

Round 11: Sc in each of next 10 sts, dec, sc in each of next 18 sts, dec, sc in each of next 8 sts. (38 sc)

Round 12: Sc in each of next 10 sts, dec, sc in each of next 17 sts, dec, sc in each of next 7 sts. (36 sc)

Round 13: [Sc in each of next 4 sts, dec] 6 times. (30 sc)

Round 14: Sc in each st around. (30 sc)

Round 15: [Sc in each of next 3 sts, dec] 6 times. (24 sc)

Round 16: Sc in each st around. (24 sc)

Rounds 17-20: *(4 rounds)* Sc in each st around. (24 sc)

Note: When attaching each Arm, flatten the top of the Arm and hold against the Body. Work the "attaching" stitches through both the layers of the Arm and the Body together. (image 16)

Round 21: *(Attaching Arms)* Sc in each of next 6 sts; working on First Arm & Body, sc in each of next 5 sts *(First Arm attached)* *(image 17)*; working on Body only, sc in each of next 8 sts; working on Second Arm & Body, sc in each of next 5 sts *(Second Arm attached)*. (24 sc)

Round 22: [Sc in each of next 2 sts, dec] 6 times. (18 sc)

Round 23: [Sc in each of next 7 sts, dec] 2 times. (16 sc)

Change to MC.

Rounds 24-25: *(Neck - 2 rounds)* Sc in each st around. (16 sc) *(image 18)*

Fasten off, leaving a long tail for sewing.

1. Finish stuffing the Body.

2. Set Body aside.

DRESS

Note: Dress is worked from top down in joined rounds.

With Color D, ch 24; taking care not to twist ch, join with sl st in first ch to form a ring.

Round 1: Ch 1, hdc in first ch, hdc in each of next 2 ch, 2 hdc in next ch, [hdc in each of next 3 ch, 2 hdc in next ch] 5 times; join with sl st to first hdc. (30 hdc) *(image 19)*

Round 2: Ch 1, hdc in same st as joining, hdc in each of next 2 sts, ch 4, skip next 6 sts *(first Armhole)*, hdc in each of next 10 sts, ch 4, skip next 6 sts *(second Armhole)*, hdc in each of next 5 sts; join with sl st to first hdc. (18 hdc & 2 ch-4 loops) *(image 20)*

Round 3: Ch 1, hdc in same st as joining, hdc each of next 2 sts; working in ch-4, 2 hdc in next ch, hdc in each of next 3 ch; 2 hdc in next st, hdc in each of next 9 sts; working in ch-4, 2 hdc in next ch, hdc in each of next 3 ch; 2 hdc in next st, hdc in each of next 4 sts; join with sl st to first hdc. (30 hdc) *(image 21)*

Round 4: Ch 1, hdc in same st as joining, hdc in each of next 3 sts, [2 hdc in next st, hdc in each of next 2 sts] 3 times, hdc in each of next 7 sts, [2 hdc in next st, hdc in each of next 2 sts] 3 times, hdc in next st; join with sl st to first sc. (36 hdc)

Round 5: Ch 1, hdc in each st around; join with sl st to first hdc. (36 hdc)

Change to larger hook.

Round 6: Ch 1, hdc in same st as joining, hdc in each of next 9 sts, 2 hdc in next st, hdc in each of next 18 sts, 2 hdc in next st, hdc in each of next 6 sts; join with sl st to first hdc. (38 hdc)

Rounds 7-8: *(2 rounds)* Ch 1, hdc in each st around; join with sl st to first hdc. (38 hdc)

Round 9: Ch 1, hdc in same st as joining, hdc in each of next 11 sts, 2 hdc in next st, hdc in each of next 19 sts, 2 hdc in next st, hdc in each of next 5 sts; join with sl st to first hdc. (40 hdc)

Rounds 10-11: *(2 rounds)* Ch 1, hdc in each st around; join with sl st to first hdc. (40 hdc)

Fasten off and weave in ends. *(image 22)*

Pocket (Make 2)

Note: Pocket is worked in rows, across both sides of starting chain.

Row 1: *(Wrong Side)* With Color E, ch 5, sc in 2nd ch from hook, sc in each of next 2 ch, 4 sc in last ch; working on other side of chain, sc in each of next 3 ch. (10 sc)

Row 2: *(Right Side)* Ch 1, turn, sc in first st, sc in each of next 2 sts, [inc in next st] 4 times, sc in each of next 3 sts. (14 sc)

Fasten off, leaving a long tail for sewing. *(image 23)*

FINISHING THE DOLL - use photos as guide

1. Using long tails and yarn needle, sew Pockets to front of Dress, over Rounds 8 through 10, and about 3 stitches apart.

2. With Color C, add several small straight stitches across top of each Pocket.

3. Place the Dress on Body. *(image 24)*

4. Using long tail and yarn needle, sew Body to Head, working through all 16 sts around Neck. *(images 25 & 26)*

TIP: *Ensure Body is centered between the Hair Buns. Maintain a wide, round Neck opening, adding extra stuffing before finishing.*

Face

TIP: *Use straight pins to mark positions of facial features, based on preferred placement.*

1. With Black Floss (using 4 to 6 strands, depending on preferred thickness), embroider Mouth over Round 10 on Face.

2. For Eyes, create arcs about 4 rounds wide and 2-3 stitches tall. *(image 27)*

3. Use 2 strands of Floss and embroider eyebrows above the eyes.

4. With Color F and yarn needle, embroider a few short, straight stitches under the outer edge of each Eye, to add Cheek markings.

Hair Clip

Row 1: With Color C, ch 21; sl st in 2nd ch from hook, sl st in each of next 19 ch. (20 sl sts)

Fasten of, leaving a long tail for sewing.

1. Use straight pins to shape the Hair Clip over Rows 9 and 10 of Hair. *(image 28)*

2. Use long tail and yarn needle to sew in place. *(image 29)*

Cactus Girls

Follow instructions for chosen Cactus Girl, referring to Basic Doll instructions when needed.

Prickly Pear   Barrel Cactus   Saguaro

About 6¾" (17 cm) tall

BASIC DOLL

BASIC DOLL HEAD

Front (Face)

Round 1: With MC, make a magic ring, 6 sc in ring. (6 sc)

Round 2: Inc in each st around. (12 sc)

Round 3: [Sc in next st, inc in next st] 6 times. (18 sc)

Round 4: [Sc in next st, inc in next st, sc in next st] 6 times. (24 sc)

Round 5: [Sc in each of next 3 sts, inc in next st] 6 times. (30 sc)

Round 6: [Sc in each of next 2 sts, inc in next st, sc in each of next 2 sts] 6 times. (36 sc)

Round 7: [Sc in each of next 5 sts, inc in next st] 6 times. (42 sc)

Round 8: [Sc in each of next 3 sts, inc in next st, sc in each of next 3 sts] 6 times. (48 sc)

Round 9: [Sc in each of next 7 sts, inc in next st] 6 times. (54 sc)

Round 10: [Sc in each of next 4 sts, inc in next st, sc in each of next 4 sts] 6 times. (60 sc)

Round 11: [Sc in each of next 9 sts, inc in next st] 6 times. (66 sc)

Rounds 12-13: *(2 rounds)* Sc in each st around. (66 sc)

Fasten off.

Back (Hair)

Rounds 1-12: *(12 Rounds)* With Color B, repeat Rounds 1-12 of Head Front (omitting last round). Do not fasten off.

Head Assembly

1. Hold the Front and Back together with right sides facing outwards. *(image 1)*

2. With Color B, single crochet in both the next stitch on Back and corresponding stitch on Front. This is the first stitch of the "Hairline". *(image 2)*

3. Working through both Back & Front together, single crochet in each of next {number for specific Doll} stitches, to complete the Hairline. *(image 3)*

4. Change to MC, and continue working single crochet stitches *(image 4)*, stuffing the Head firmly before finishing the round. *(image 5)*

5. Join the round with a slip stitch in the first single crochet stitch.

6. Fasten off and weave in ends. *(image 6)*

BASIC DOLL ARM (Make 2)

Round 1: With MC, make a magic ring, 6 sc in ring. (6 sc)

Round 2: [Sc in next st, inc in each st] 3 times. (9 sc)

Rounds 3-15: *(13 rounds)* Sc in each st around. (9 sc)

Round 16: Dec, sc in each of next 7 sts. (8 sc)

Fasten off.

1. Stuff the lower third of each Arm, leaving the remainder of Arm unstuffed.

2. Set Arms aside.

BASIC DOLL LEGS & BODY

First Leg

Round 1: With MC, make a magic ring, 6 sc in ring. (6 sc)

Round 2: Inc in each st around. (12 sc)

Rounds 3-12: *(10 rounds)* Sc in each st around. (12 sc)

Fasten off.

Second Leg

Rounds 1-12: *(12 rounds)* With MC, repeat Rounds 1-12 of First Leg. Do not fasten off. Continue with Body.

Body

Round 1: *(Joining Legs)* From Second Leg, ch 3; working on First Leg, sc in next st *(image 7)*, sc in each of next 11 sts; working in ch-3, sc in each of next 3 ch; working on Second Leg, sc in each of next 12 sts; working on other side of ch-3, sc in each of next 3 ch. (30 sc)

Round 2: Sc in each of next 6 sts, inc in next st, sc in each of next 14 sts, inc in next st, sc in each of next 8 sts. (32 sc) *(image 8)*

Round 3: [Sc in each of next 7 sts, inc in next st] 4 times. (36 sc)

Rounds 4-6: *(3 rounds)* Sc in each st around. (36 sc)

Stuff the Legs.

Round 7: Sc in each of next 7 sts, dec, sc in each of next 17 sts, dec, sc in each of next 8 sts. (34 sc)

Round 8: Sc in each st around. (34 sc)

Round 9: Sc in each of next 7 sts, dec, sc in each of next 16 sts, dec, sc in each of next 7 sts. (32 sc)

Round 10: Sc in each st around. (32 sc)

Round 11: Sc in each of next 7 sts, dec, sc in each of next 15 sts, dec, sc in each of next 6 sts. (30 sc)

Round 12: [Sc in each of next 3 sts, dec] 6 times. (24 sc)

Round 13: Sc in each st around. (24 sc)

Round 14: [Sc in each of next 2 sts, dec, sc in each of next 2 sts] 4 times. (20 sc)

Round 15: Sc in each st around. (20 sc)

Round 16: [Sc in each of next 3 sts, dec] 4 times. (16 sc)

Place Cactus Dress on Body before continuing. *(image 9)*

Start stuffing Body.

Note: *When attaching each Arm, flatten the top of the Arm and hold against the Body. Work the "attaching" stitches through both the layers of the Arm and the Body together.*

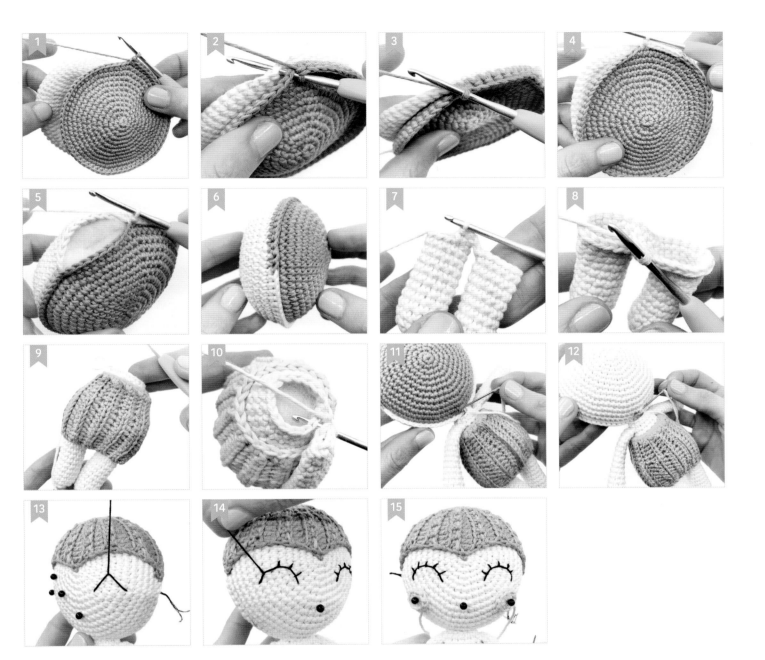

Round 17: *(Attaching Arms)* Sc in each of next 3 sts; working on First Arm & Body, sc in each of next 4 sts *(image 10) (First Arm attached)*; working on Body only, sc in each of next 5 sts; working on Second Arm & Body, sc in each of next 4 sts *(Second Arm attached)*. (16 sc)

Round 18: *(Neck)* Sc in each of next 4 sts, dec, sc in each of next 7 sts, dec, sc in next st. (14 sc)

Fasten off, leaving a long tail for sewing.

BASIC DOLL ASSEMBLY

1. Finish stuffing the Body.

2. Using long tail and yarn needle, sew Body to Head, working through all 14 stitches around Neck. *(images 11 & 12)*

TIP: *Ensure Body is centered between ends of Hairline. Maintain a wide, round Neck opening, adding extra stuffing before finishing.*

BASIC FACE - use photos as guide

TIP: *Use straight pins to mark positions of facial features, based on preferred placement.*

1. With Black Floss (using 4 to 6 strands, depending on preferred thickness), embroider Mouth over Round 7 on Face.

2. For Eyes, create arcs about 4 rounds wide and 2-3 stitches tall. *(images 13 & 14)*

Cheek (Make 2)

Round 1: With Color A, make a magic ring, ch 2 *(does not count as a stitch)*, 9 hdc in ring, join with sl st to first hdc. (9 hdc)

Fasten off, leaving long tail for sewing.

1. Using long tail and yarn needle, sew Cheeks to either side of face, in line with the Mouth and below outer edge of each Eye. *(image 15)*

Bess

THE BARREL CACTUS

MATERIALS & TOOLS

YARN: HELLO Cotton

- **Main Color (MC):** Seashell (161) for Face, Arms, Legs & Body
- **Color A:** Salmon (109) for Cheeks
- **Color B:** Sea Green (136) for Hair & Dress
- **Color C:** Dark Yellow (120) for Flower and Dress Trim

HOOK SIZE: 2.5 mm hook

OTHER: DMC Embroidery Floss - Black for Eyes and Mouth
Embroidery Needle
Stitch Marker
Yarn Needle
Stuffing
Straight Pins

BESS

HEAD

Follow instructions for Basic Doll Head - Front & Back.

Head Assembly

Follow Steps 1-6 of Basic Doll Head Assembly, and in Step 3, single crochet in each of next 34 stitches to complete the Hairline. (35 stitches)

ARMS

Follow instructions for Basic Doll Arm - Make 2.

DRESS

Row 1: *(Right Side)* With Color B, ch 16, sc in 2nd ch from hook, sc in each of next 14 ch. (15 sc)

Row 2: Ch 1, turn, working in back loops only, sc in each of first 5 sts, hdc in each of next 7 sts, sc in each of next 3 sts. (15 sts)

Row 3: Ch 1, turn, working in back loops only, sc in each of first 3 sts, hdc in each of next 7 sts, sc in each of next 5 sts. (15 sts)

Row 4: Ch 1, turn, working in back loops only, sc in each of first 5 sts, hdc in each of next 7 sts, sc in each of next 3 sts. (15 sts)

Rows 5-24: *(20 rows)* Repeat Rows 3-4 another 10 times. *(image 1)*

Row 25: *(Joining Row)* Ch 1, turn, fold Dress so that Row 1 is behind Row 24; matching stitches, work through back loops of last row and starting chain stitches together, sc in each of the 15 stitches across. *(image 2)*

Change to Color C.

Round 1: *(Dress Trim)* Ch 1, working in row ends, sc in each of next 24 rows; join with sl st to first sc. (24 sc) *(image 3)*

Fasten off and weave in ends.

LEGS & BODY

Follow instructions for Basic Doll Legs and Body, placing Dress on Body before joining the Arms on Round 17. *(image 4)*

DOLL ASSEMBLY

Follow Basic Doll Assembly Instructions.

FACE

Follow Basic Face instructions.

HAIR

Note: Hair is worked as a single piece in rows, starting with a magic ring.

Crown

Row A: *(Right Side)* With Color B, make a magic ring; ch 3 *(counts as first dc, now and throughout)*, 5 dc in ring. (6 dc) Tighten ring but do not join round.

Row B: Ch 3, turn, dc in first st, 2 dc in each of next 4 sts, skip last st *(do not work in top of ch-3)*. (10 dc) Do not fasten off.

Hair Bangs

Note: Slip stitches in Crown Row B are for securing the rows and are not counted as a stitch, nor included in the stitch count.

Row 1: *(Right Side)* Turn, ch 14 *(image 5)*, sl st in 2nd ch from hook, sc in next ch, dc in each of next 7 ch, hdc in each of next 2 ch, sc in each of next 2 ch; working in Crown Row B, skip first st, sl st in next st *(to secure Bangs)*. (13 sts) *(image 6)*

Row 2: Ch 1, turn, working in front loops only, *(skip sl st)*, sc in each of next 10 sts *(image 7)*, dec *(using next 2 sts)*, skip last sl st. (11 sc)

Row 3: Ch 2 *(does NOT count as first st, now and throughout)*, turn, skip first st, working in back loops only, dc in each of next 6 sts, hdc in each of next 2 sts, sc in each of next 2 sts; working in Crown Row B, sl st in both loops of next st. (10 sts)

Row 4: Ch 1, turn, working in front loops only, sc in each of next 8 sts, dec *(using last 2 sts)*. (9 sc)

Row 5: Ch 2, turn, working in back loops only, dc in first st, dc in each of next 4 sts, hdc in each of next 2 sts, sc in each of next 2 sts; working in Crown Row B, sl st in both loops of next st. (9 sts)

Row 6: Ch 1, turn, working in front loops only, sc in each st across. (9 sc)

Row 7: Ch 3 *(counts as first dc, now and throughout)*, turn, working in back loops only, dc in first st, dc in each of next 4 sts, hdc in each of next 2 sts, sc in each of next 2 sts; working in Crown Row B, sl st in both loops of next st. (10 sts)

Row 8: Ch 1, turn, working in front loops only, sc in first st, sc in each of next 8 sts, inc in last st *(3rd ch of ch-3)*. (11 sc)

Row 9: Ch 2, turn, skip first st, working in back loops only, dc in each of next 6 sts, hdc in each of next 2 sts, sc in

each of next 2 sts; working in Crown Row B, sl st in both loops of next st. (10 sts)

Rows 10-14: Repeat Rows 4-8 once.

Row 15: Ch 3, turn, working in back loops only, dc in first st, dc in each of next 6 sts, hdc in each of next 2 sts, sc in each of next 2 sts; working in Crown Row B, sl st in both loops of next st. (12 sts)

Row 16: Ch 1, turn, working in front loops only, sc in each of next 11 sts, inc in last st *(3rd ch of ch-3)*. (13 sc)

Fasten off, leaving a long tail for sewing. *(image 8)*

1. Position Hair on Head Front, gently shaping to fit full length of Hairline, and securing with pins. *(image 9)*.

2. Using the long tail and yarn needle, sew the Hair in place along the Hairline. *(image 10)*

3. Sew a small stitch to secure the tip of Hair Bangs (Row 9) to center of Face.

4. With Color C, make a series of vertical running stitches along every second row of Hair Bangs, using pictures as a guide.

FLOWER

Round 1: With Color C, make a magic ring; 7 sc in ring. (7 sc) Do not join.

Round 2: Working in back loops only, sc in each st around; join with sl st to first sc. (7 sts)

Round 3: *(Large Petals)* [Ch 6, sl st in 2nd ch from hook, sc in next ch, hdc in each of next 3 ch; working on Round 2, sl st in next st] 6 times, ch 6, sl st in 2nd ch from hook, sc in next ch, hdc in each of next 3 ch; sl st in first unworked front loop on Round 1. (7 Petals)

Round 4: *(Small Petals)* [Ch 5, sl st in 2nd ch from hook, sc in next ch, hdc in each of next 2 ch; sl st in next unworked front loop on Round 1] 6 times. (6 Petals)

Fasten off, leaving a long tail for sewing.

1. Use yarn needle to sew Flower to top of Hair. *(images 11 & 12)*

Pia

THE PRICKLY PEAR

MATERIALS & TOOLS

YARN: HELLO Cotton

- **Main Color (MC):** Seashell (161) for Face, Arms, Legs & Body
- **Color A:** Salmon (109) for Cheeks
- **Color B:** Sage (137) for Hair & Dress
- **Color C:** Coral (111) for Flower
- **Color D:** Off-white (155) small amount for Hair

HOOK SIZE: 2.5 mm hook

OTHER: DMC Embroidery Floss - Black for Eyes and Mouth

Embroidery Needle

Stitch Marker

Yarn Needle

Stuffing

Straight Pins

PIA

HEAD

Follow instructions for Basic Doll Head - Front & Back.

Head Assembly

Follow Steps 1-6 of Basic Doll Head Assembly, and in Step 3, single crochet in each of next 50 stitches to complete the Hairline. (51 stitches)

ARMS

Follow instructions for Basic Doll Arm - Make 2.

DRESS

Note: *Dress is worked from top down.*

With Color B, ch 24; taking care not to twist ch, join with sl st in first ch to form a ring.

Round 1: Ch 1, sc in same st as joining, sc in each of next 23 ch. (24 sc)

Work in continuous rounds - without joining.

Round 2: [Sc in each of next 3 sts, inc in next st] 6 times. (30 sc)

Round 3: [Sc in each of next 2 sts, inc in next st, sc in each of next 2 sts] 6 times. (36 sc)

Round 4: Sc in each st around. (36 sc)

Round 5: [Sc in each of next 5 sts, inc in next st] 6 times. (42 sc)

Round 6: Sc in each st around. (42 sc)

Round 7: [Sc in each of next 3 sts, inc in next st, sc in each of next 3 sts] 6 times. (48 sc)

Rounds 8-10: *(3 rounds)* Sc in each st around. (48 sts)

Round 11: [Sc in each of next 4 sts, dec] 8 times. (40 sc)

Round 12: [Sc in each of next 6 sts, dec] 5 times. (35 sc)

Round 13: [Sc in each of next 5 sts, dec] 5 times. (30 sc)

Round 14: Sl st in each st around. (30 sl sts)

Fasten off and weave in ends.

LEGS & BODY

Follow instructions for Basic Doll Legs and Body, placing Dress on Body before joining the Arms on Round 17. *(image 1)*

DOLL ASSEMBLY

Follow Basic Doll Assembly Instructions.

FACE

Follow Basic Face instructions.

HAIR

Note: *The Hair is worked in two pieces - an Outer Hair Band which is secured to the Hairline, and Hair Bangs.*

Outer Hair Band

Row 1: *(Wrong Side)* With Color B, ch 52, sl st in 2nd ch from hook, sc in each of next 49 ch, sl st in last ch. (49 sc & 2 sl sts)

Row 2: *(Right Side)* Turn, skip first sl st, [sc in each of next 3 sts, dec] 9 times, sc in each of next 3 sts, sl st in next st. (39 sc & 1 sl st) Leave remaining sl st unworked.

Row 3: Turn, skip first sl st, sl st in next st, sc in each of next 8 sts, dc in each of next 20 sts, sc in each of next 8 sts, sl st in next st. (16 sc, 20 dc & 2 sl sts) Leave remaining st unworked.

Fasten off, leaving a long tail for sewing. *(image 2)*

1. Align the starting chain of Outer Hair Band along the Hairline, with Row 3 across the forehead.

2. Use long tail and yarn needle to sew the starting chain to Hairline. *(image 3)*

Hair Bangs

Row 1: *(Right Side)* With Color B, make a magic ring; ch 3 *(counts as first dc, now and throughout)*, 5 dc in ring. (6 dc) Tighten ring but do not join round.

Row 2: Ch 3, turn, dc in first st, 2 dc in each of next 4 sts, 2 dc in last st *(3rd ch of ch-3)*. (12 dc)

Row 3: Ch 3, turn, dc in first st, dc in each of next 2 sts, sc in each of next 6 sts, dc in each of next 2 sts, 2 dc in last st. (8 dc & 6 sc)

Row 4: Ch 3, turn, dc in first st, dc in each of next 2 sts, sc in each of next 8 sts, dc in each of next 2 sts, 2 dc in last st. (8 dc & 8 sc)

Row 5: Ch 3, turn, dc in first st, dc in each of next 14 sts, 2 dc in last st. (18 dc)

Fasten off, leaving a long tail for sewing. *(image 4)*

1. Position Hair Bangs on Head Front, below Outer Hair Band. *(image 5)*

2. Use long tail and yarn needle, sew Hair Bangs securely to Row 3 Outer Hair Band. *(image 6)*

Cactus Pads

Note: *The Pads are worked in rows, across both sides of the starting chain.*

Large Pad (Make 2)

Row 1: *(Right Side)* With Color B, ch 9, sc in 2nd ch from hook, sc in each of next 2 ch, dc in each of next 4 ch, 8 dc in last ch; working on other side of starting ch, dc in each of next 4 ch, sc in each of next 3 ch. (6 sc & 16 dc)

Row 2: Ch 1, turn, sc in first st, sc in each of next 7 sts, [inc in next st] 6 times, sc in each of next 8 sts. (28 sc)

Fasten off, leaving a long tail on one Pad. Weave in ends on other Pad

Medium Pad (Make 2)

Row 1: *(Right Side)* With Color B, ch 6, sc in 2nd ch from hook, sc in next ch, dc in each of next 2 ch, 8 dc in last ch; working on other side of starting ch, dc in each of next 2 ch, sc in each of next 2 ch. (4 sc & 12 dc)

Row 2: Ch 1, turn, sc in each of next 6 sts, [inc in next st] 4 times, sc in each of next 6 sts. (20 sc)

Fasten off, leaving a long tail on one Pad. Weave in ends on other Pad

Small Pad (Make 2)

Row 1: *(Right Side)* With Color B, ch 4, sc in 2nd ch from hook, hdc in next ch, 8 dc in last ch; working on other side of starting ch, hdc in next ch, sc in next ch. (2 sc, 2 hdc & 8 dc)

Fasten off, leaving a long tail on one Pad. Weave in ends on other Pad

1. With right sides facing outwards, using long tails and yarn needle, sew each pair of Cactus Pads together. *(image 7)* Pads do not need to be stuffed.

2. Sew Small Pad to top edge of Large Pad (use photo as guide).

3. With Color D, embroider a few small "V"-shaped straight stitches on one side of each pad to create "spines". *(image 8)*

4. Position Large and Medium Pad on top of Head, placed just behind the Hairline, and sew in place.

5. Embroider additional "spines" on the Hair Bangs and Outer Band.

FLOWER

Round 1: With Color C, make a magic ring; 6 sc in ring; join with sl st to back loop of first sc. (6 sts)

Round 2: *(Large Petals)* [Ch 4, sc in 2nd ch from hook, hdc in each of next 2 ch; sl st in back loop of next st on Round 1] 5 times, ch 4, sc in 2nd ch from hook, hdc in each of next 2 ch; sl st in unworked front loop of first st on Round 1. (6 Petals) *(image 9)*

Round 3: *(Small Petals)* [Ch 3, sc in 2nd ch from hook, hdc in next ch, sl st in unworked front loop of next st on Round 1] 5 times, ch 3, sc in 2nd ch from hook, hdc in next ch, sl st in base of first Petal. (6 Petals)

Fasten off, leaving a long tail for sewing.

1. Use a yarn needle to sew Flower to top of Head. *(images 10 & 11)*

Sadie

THE SAGUARO

MATERIALS & TOOLS

YARN: HELLO Cotton

- **Main Color (MC):** Seashell (161) for Face, Arms, Legs & Body
- **Color A:** Salmon (109) for Cheeks
- **Color B:** Light Green (129) for Hair & Dress
- **Color C:** Berry (108) for Flower

HOOK SIZE: 2.5 mm hook

OTHER: DMC Embroidery Floss -Black for Eyes and Mouth

Embroidery Needle

Stitch Marker

Yarn Needle

Stuffing

Straight Pins

SADIE

HEAD

Follow instructions for Basic Doll Head - Front & Back.

Head Assembly

Follow Steps 1-6 of Basic Doll Head Assembly, and in Step 3, single crochet in each of next 39 stitches to complete the Hairline. (40 stitches)

ARMS

Follow instructions for Basic Doll Arm - Make 2.

DRESS

Row 1: *(Right Side)* With Color B, ch 16, sc in 2nd ch from hook, sc in each of next 14 ch. (15 sc)

Row 2: Ch 1, turn, working in back loops only, sc in each of first 5 sts, hdc in each of next 7 sts, sc in each of next 3 sts. (15 sts)

Row 3: Ch 1, turn, working in back loops only, sc in each of first 3 sts, hdc in each of next 7 sts, sc in each of next 5 sts. (15 sts)

Row 4: Ch 1, turn, working in back loops only, sc in each of first 5 sts, hdc in each of next 7 sts, sc in each of next 3 sts. (15 sts)

Rows 5-24: *(20 rows)* Repeat Rows 3-4 another 10 times.

Row 25: *(Joining Row)* Ch 1, turn, fold Dress so that Row 1 is behind Row 24 *(image 1)*; matching stitches, work through back loops of last row and starting chain stitches together, sc in each of the 15 stitches across *(image 2)*.

Round 1: *(Dress Trim)* Ch 1, working in row ends, sc in each of next 24 rows; join with sl st to first sc. (24 sc)

Fasten off and weave in ends.

LEGS & BODY

Follow instructions for Basic Doll Legs and Body, placing Dress on Body before joining the Arms on Round 17. *(image 3)*

DOLL ASSEMBLY

Follow Basic Doll Assembly Instructions.

FACE

Follow Basic Face instructions.

HAIR

Note: Hair is worked as a single piece in rows, starting with a magic ring.

Crown

Row A: *(Right Side)* With Color B, make a magic ring; ch 3 *(counts as first dc, now and throughout)*, 5 dc in ring. (6 dc) Tighten ring but do not join round.

Row B: Ch 3, turn, dc in first st, 2 dc in each of next 4 sts, skip last st *(do not work in top of ch-3)*. (10 dc)

Hair Bangs

Note: Slip stitches in Crown Row B are for securing the rows and are not counted as a stitch, nor included in the stitch count.

Row 1: *(Right Side)* Turn, ch 17, sl st in 2ⁿᵈ ch from hook, sc in next ch, dc in each of next 10 ch, hdc in each of next 2 ch, sc in each of next 2 ch; working in Crown Row B, skip first st, sl st in next st *(to secure Bangs)* (16 sts)

Row 2: Ch 1, turn, working in front loops only, *(skip sl st)*, sc in each of next 13 sts, dec *(using next 2 sts)*, skip last sl st. (14 sc)

Row 3: Ch 2 *(does NOT count as first st, now and throughout)*, turn, skip first st, working in back loops only, dc in each of next 9 sts, hdc in each of next 2 sts, sc in each of next 2 sts; working in Crown Row B, sl st in both loops of next st. (13 sts)

Row 4: Ch 1, turn, working in front loops only, sc in each of next 11 sts, dec *(using last 2 sts)*. (12 sc)

Row 5: Ch 2, turn, working in back loops only, skip first st, dc in each of next 7 sts, hdc in each of next 2 sts, sc in each of next 2 sts; working in Crown Row B, sl st in both loops of next st. (11 sts)

Row 6: Ch 1, turn, working in front loops only, sc in each of next 9 sts, dec *(using last 2 sts)*. (10 sc)

Row 7: Ch 3 *(counts as first dc, now and throughout)*, turn, working in back loops only, dc in first st, dc in each of next 4 sts, hdc in each of next 2 sts, sc in each of next 2 sts; working in Crown Row B, sl st in both loops of next st. (10 sts)

Row 8: Ch 1, turn, working in front loops only, sc in first st, each of next 8 sts, sc in last st *(3ʳᵈ ch of ch-3)*. (10 sc)

Row 9: Ch 3, turn, working in back loops only, dc in each of next 5 sts, hdc in each of next 2 sts, sc in each of next 2 sts; working in Crown Row B, sl st in both loops of next st. (10 sts)

Row 10: Ch 1, turn, working in front loops only, sc in first st, each of next 8 sts, inc in last st *(3ʳᵈ ch of ch-3)*. (11 sc)

Row 11: Ch 3, turn, working in back loops only, dc in each of next 6 sts, hdc in each of next 2 sts, sc in each of next 2 sts; working in Crown Row B, sl st in both loops of next st. (11 sts)

Row 12: Ch 1, turn, working in front loops only, sc in first st, each of next 9 sts, inc in last st *(3ʳᵈ ch of ch-3)*. (12 sc)

Row 13: Ch 3, turn, working in back loops only, dc in first st, dc in each of next 7 sts, hdc in each of next 2 sts, sc in each of next 2 sts; working in Crown Row B, sl st in both loops of next st. (13 sts)

Row 14: Ch 1, turn, working in front loops only, sc in first st, each of next 11 sts, inc in last st *(3ʳᵈ ch of ch-3)*. (14 sc)

Row 15: Ch 3, turn, working in back loops only, dc in first st, dc in each of next 9 sts, hdc in each of next 2 sts, sc in each of next 2 sts; working in Crown Row B, sl st in both loops of next st. (15 sts)

Row 16: Ch 1, turn, working in front loops only, sc in first st, each of next 13 sts, inc in last st *(3ʳᵈ ch of ch-3)*. (16 sc)

Fasten off, leaving a long tail for sewing.

1. Position Hair on Head Front, gently shaping to fit full length of Hairline, and securing with pins. *(image 4)*

2. Using the long tail and yarn needle, sew the Hair in place along the Hairline. *(image 5)*

3. With Color C, make three rows of running stitches along the Hair Bangs, using pictures as a guide.

Cactus Arms (Make 2)

Round 1: With Color B, starting with a long tail, make a magic ring, 6 sc in ring. (6 sc)

Round 2: Inc in each st around. (12 sc)

Round 3: [Sc in next st, inc in next st] 6 times. (18 sc) *(image 6)*

Round 4: Skip next 9 sts, *(fold work to insert hook from right side)* sc in next st *(image 7)*, sc in each of next 8 sts. (9 sc)

Rounds 5-8: *(4 rounds)* Sc in each st around. (9 sc)

Round 9: [Sc in next st, dec] 3 times. (6 sc)

Fasten off, leaving a long tail for sewing.

1. With yarn needle, weave tail through front loop of each stitch on last round and pull tight to close hole. *(image 8)*

2. Lightly stuff Cactus Arms.

3. Position Cactus Arms on either side of Head (over first and last two rows of Hair Bangs), with the skipped stitches from Round 3 against the Head.

4. Using starting tails, sew around each skipped stitch, to secure the Cactus Arms to the Head. *(image 9)*

FLOWER

Round 1: With Color C, make a magic ring; 6 sc in ring; join with sl st to back loop of first sc. (6 sts)

Round 2: *(Large Petals)* [Ch 4, sc in 2nd ch from hook, hdc in each of next 2 ch; sl st in back loop of next st on Round 1] 5 times, ch 4, sc in 2nd ch from hook, hdc in each of next 2 ch; sl st in unworked front loop of first st on Round 1. (6 Petals)

Round 3: *(Small Petals)* [Ch 3, sc in 2nd ch from hook, hdc in next ch, sl st in unworked front loop of next st on Round 1] 5 times, ch 3, sc in 2nd ch from hook, hdc in next ch, sl st in base of first Petal. (6 Petals)

Fasten off, leaving a long tail for sewing.

1. Use a yarn needle to sew Flower to top of Head. *(images 10 & 11)*

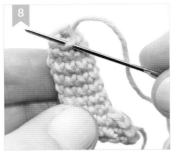

Animals
Crocodile · Giraffe · Lion

Follow instructions for chosen Animal, referring to Basic Doll instructions when needed.

Crocodile   Giraffe   Lion

SPECIAL STITCHES & TECHNIQUES

Single Crochet Spike Stitch (sc-sp)

Insert hook in specified stitch one round below current round, pull up loop to height of stitches in current round, yarn over and draw through both loops on hook. (single crochet spike stitch made)

BASIC DOLL

HEAD

Front (Face)

Round 1: With MC, make a magic ring, 6 sc in ring. (6 sc)

Round 2: Inc in each st around. (12 sc)

Round 3: [Sc in next st, inc in next st] 6 times. (18 sc)

Round 4: [Sc in next st, inc in next st, sc in next st] 6 times. (24 sc)

Round 5: [Sc in each of next 3 sts, inc in next st] 6 times. (30 sc)

Round 6: [Sc in each of next 2 sts, inc in next st, sc in each of next 2 sts] 6 times. (36 sc)

Round 7: [Sc in each of next 5 sts, inc in next st] 6 times. (42 sc)

Round 8: [Sc in each of next 3 sts, inc in next st, sc in each of next 3 sts] 6 times. (48 sc)

Round 9: [Sc in each of next 7 sts, inc in next st] 6 times. (54 sc)

Round 10: [Sc in each of next 4 sts, inc in next st, sc in each of next 4 sts] 6 times. (60 sc)

Round 11: [Sc in each of next 9 sts, inc in next st] 6 times. (66 sc)

Round 12: Sc in each st around. (66 sc)

Fasten off.

Back (Hood)

Rounds 1-12: *(12 Rounds)* With Color A, repeat Rounds 1-12 of Head Front

Round 13: Sc in each st around. (66 sc) Do not fasten off. Continue with Head Assembly.

Head Assembly

1. Hold the Front and Back together with right sides facing outwards, and Front of Head facing you. *(image 1)*

2. With Color A, insert hook in both the next stitch on Front and corresponding stitch on Back *(image 2)* and work a single crochet stitch. This is the first stitch of the "Hoodline".

3. Working through both the Front & Back together, single crochet in each of next 65 stitches to complete the Hoodline (66 stitches) *(image 3)*, stuffing Head firmly before finishing the round. *(image 4)*

4. Join the round with a slip stitch in the first single crochet stitch. *(image 5)*

5. Fasten off and weave in ends.

ARM (Make 2)

Round 1: With MC, make a magic ring, 6 sc in ring. (6 sc)

Round 2: Inc in each st around. (12 sc)

Rounds 3-4: *(2 rounds)* Sc in each st around. (12 sc)

Round 5: Sc in each of next 6 sts, [dec] 3 times. (9 sc)

Rounds 6-14: *(9 rounds)* Sc in each st around. (9 sc)

Round 15: Dec, sc in each of next 7 sts. (8 sc) Sc in each of next 3 sts *(to position decreases on outer Arm)*.

Fasten off.

1. Stuff the lower third of each Arm, leaving the remainder of Arm unstuffed.

2. Set Arms aside.

LEGS & BODY

First Leg

Round 1: With MC, make a magic ring, 6 sc in ring. (6 sc)

Round 2: Inc in each st around. (12 sc)

Rounds 3-12: *(10 rounds)* Sc in each st around. (12 sc)

Fasten off.

Second Leg

Rounds 1-12: *(12 rounds)* With MC, repeat Rounds 1-12 of First Leg.

Change to Color A. Continue with Body.

Body

Round 1: *(Joining Legs)* From Second Leg *(with Color A)*, ch 3; working on First Leg, sc in next st *(image 6)*, sc in each of next 11 sts; working in ch-3, sc in each of next 3 ch; working on Second Leg, sc in each of next 12 sts; working on other side of ch-3, sc in each of next 3 ch. (30 sc)

Round 2: Sc in each of next 6 sts, inc in next st, sc in each of next 14 sts, inc in next st, sc in each of next 8 sts. (32 sc)

Round 3: [Sc in each of next 3 sts, inc in next st] 8 times. (40 sc)

Stuff the Legs. *(image 7)*

Rounds 4-8: *(5 rounds)* Sc in each st around. (40 sc)

Round 9: Sc in each of next 8 sts, dec, sc in each of next 18 sts, dec, sc in each of next 10 sts. (38 sc)

Round 10: Sc in each of next 8 sts, dec, sc in each of next 17 sts, dec, sc in each of next 9 sts. (36 sc)

Round 11: [Sc in each of next 4 sts, dec] 6 times. (30 sc)

Rounds 12-13: *(2 rounds)* Sc in each st around. (30 sc)

Round 14: [Sc in each of next 3 sts, dec] 6 times. (24 sc)

Round 15: Sc in each st around. (24 sc)

Start stuffing Body.

Round 16: [Sc in each of next 4 sts, dec] 4 times. (20 sc)

Note: When attaching each Arm, flatten the top of the Arm and hold against the Body with the decrease stitches on Arm Round 5 facing outwards (image 8). Work the "attaching" stitches through both the layers of the Arm and the Body together.

Round 17: *(Attaching Arms)* Sc in each of next 4 sts; working on First Arm & Body, sc in each of next 4 sts *(First Arm attached)*; working on Body only, sc in each of next 8 sts; working on Second Arm & Body, sc in each of next 4 sts *(image 9)* *(Second Arm attached)*. (20 sc)

Round 18: Sc in each of next 4 sts, [dec] 2 times, sc in each of next 8 sts, [dec] 2 times. (16 sc)

Round 19: *(Neck)* Sc in each st around. (16 sc) *(image 10)*

Fasten off, leaving a long tail for sewing.

DOLL ASSEMBLY

1. Finish stuffing the Body.

2. Using long tail and yarn needle, sew Body to Head, working through all 16 sts around Neck. *(images 11-13)*

TIP: Maintain a wide, round Neck opening, adding extra stuffing before finishing.

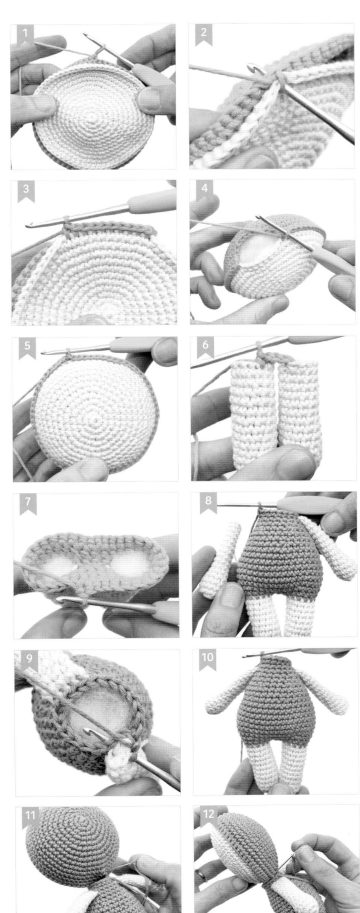

BASIC HOOD

Row 1: *(Wrong Side)* With Color A, ch 36, sc in 2nd ch from hook, sc in each of next 34 ch. (35 sc)

Row 2: *(Right Side)* Ch 1, turn, skip first st, dec *(using next 2 sts)*, [sc in each of next 4 sts, dec, sc in each of next 4 sts] 3 times, dec *(using last 2 sts)*. (29 sc)

Row 3: Ch 1, turn, skip first st, dec, sc in each of next 24 sts, dec. (26 sc)

Row 4: Ch 1, turn, skip first st, dec, sc in each of next 3 sts, [dec, sc in each of next 5 sts] 2 times, dec, sc in each of next 2 sts, dec. (20 sc)

Row 5: Ch 1, turn, skip first st, dec, sc in each of next 15 sts, dec. (17 sc)

Row 6: Ch 1, turn, skip first st, sc in each of next 3 sts, [dec, sc in each of next 2 sts] 3 times, sl st into last st. (13 sts) *(image 14)*

Fasten off and weave in ends.

Edging: With right side facing, attach Color A to end of Row 1, working in sides of rows, 2 sc in same row, sc in each of next 5 rows *(image 15)*; working across Row 6, sc-sp in first st, sc in each of the next 11 sts, sc-sp in last st *(image 16)*; working in sides of rows, sc in each of next 5 row, 2 sc in Row 1. (27 sc) *(image 17)*

Fasten off, leaving a long tail for sewing. *(image 18)*

1. Position the Hood, centered at top of Head. Gently stretch the Hood to fit around Face, and pin in place. *(image 19)*

2. Use long tail and yarn needle to whipstitch the starting chain of Hood to Hoodline. *(image 20)*

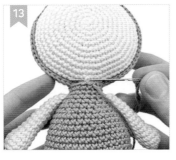
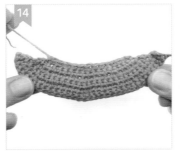
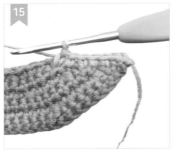

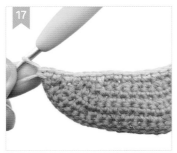

Emma

About 6¾" (17 cm) tall

THE CROCODILE

MATERIALS & TOOLS

YARN: HELLO Cotton

Main Color (MC): Misty Rose (163) for Face, Arms & Legs

Color A: Sage (137) for Bodysuit & Hood

Color B: Light Green (129) for Belly, Eyes and Scales

Color C: Off-white (155) for Teeth

Color D: Dark Brown (127) small amount for Crocodile Eyes

Color E: Salmon (109) small amount for Cheeks

HOOK SIZE: 2.5 mm hook
2.0 mm hook for Belly, Teeth and Scales

OTHER: DMC Embroidery Floss - Black for Eyes and Mouth
Embroidery Needle
Stitch Marker
Yarn Needle
Stuffing
Straight Pins

EMMA

HEAD

Follow instructions for Basic Doll Head - Front, Back & Head Assembly.

ARMS

Follow instructions for Basic Doll Arm - Make 2.

LEGS & BODY

Follow instructions for Basic Doll Legs and Body, joining the Arms on Round 17.

DOLL ASSEMBLY

Follow Basic Doll Assembly Instructions.

HOOD

Follow instructions for Basic Hood.

FACE - use photos as guide (image 1)

TIP: *Use straight pins to mark positions of facial features, based on preferred placement.*

1. With Black Floss (using 4 to 6 strands, depending on preferred thickness), embroider Mouth over Round 8 on Face.

2. For Eyes, embroider several vertical straight stitches (over 2 stitches each).

3. Use 2 strands of Floss to embroider eyebrows.

4. With Color E, embroider a few short, straight stitches under the outer edge of each Eye for Cheeks.

SNOUT

Round 1: With MC, ch 6; inc in 2nd ch from hook, sc in each of next 3 ch, 4 sc in last ch, working on other side of starting ch, sc in each of next 3 ch, inc in last ch. (14 sc)

Rounds 2-3: *(2 rounds)* Sc in each st around. (14 sc)

Round 4: [Inc in next st, sc in each of next 6 sts] 2 times. (16 sc)

Rounds 5-7: *(3 rounds)* Sc in each st around. (16 sc)

Round 8: Sc in each of next 2 sts, inc in next st, sc in each of next 7 sts, inc in next st, sc in each of next 5 sts. (18 sc)

Round 9-11: *(3 rounds)* Sc in each st around. (18 sc)

Round 12: Sc in each of next 2 sts, inc in next st, sc in each of next 8 sts, inc in next st, sc in each of next 6 sts. (20 sc)

Round 13: Sc in each st around. (20 sc)

Round 14: Sc in each st around. (20 sc) Sc in each of next 4 sts *(to move the end of round to the side of Snout).*

Joining Row: Flatten Snout, skip first st, working through both sides *(to close opening)*, sc in each of next 9 sts, skip last st.

Fasten off, leaving a long tail for sewing.

1. With Color B and yarn needle, using small straight stitches, embroider a series of V-shaped "scales" on front of Snout.

Teeth

Note: Use surface crochet along either side of Snout to create Teeth, skipping the last round of the Snout.

Row 1: With Color C and smaller hook, with front of Snout facing you, insert hook under edge stitch *(image 2)* and pull up a loop, [ch 3, sc in 3rd ch from hook, skip next 2 rounds, sl st under next round] 4 times. (4 Teeth) *(images 3 & 4)*

Fasten off and weave in ends.

Repeat Row 1 on other side of Snout.

1. Using long tail from Snout and yarn needle, sew Snout to center of Hood, securing at the Hoodline and center of face. *(image 5)*

CROCODILE EYES

Note: Eyes are worked in rows, starting with a magic ring.

Front (Make 2)

Row 1: *(Wrong Side)* With Color B, make a magic ring, ch 2, 6 hdc in ring. (6 hdc)

Tighten ring but do not join round.

Change to Color A

Row 2: *(Right Side)* Ch 1, turn, inc in each st across. (12 sc)

Fasten off and weave in ends.

1. With Color D and yarn needle, embroider eyelids across Row 1, using picture as guide. *(image 6)*

Back (Make 2)

Row 1: *(Wrong Side)* With Color A, make a magic ring, ch 2, 6 hdc in ring. (6 hdc) Tighten ring but do not join round.

Row 2: *(Right Side)* Ch 1, turn, inc in each st across. (12 sc)

Fasten off, leaving a long tail for sewing.

1. Hold a Front and Back piece together with right sides facing outwards.

2. Use long tail and yarn needle to sew pieces together.

3. Continue using yarn tail to sew Eyes to top of Head, positioned at an angle on either side of Snout. *(images 7 & 8)*

BELLY

Row 1: *(Wrong Side)* With Color B and smaller hook, ch 6, sc in 2nd ch from hook, sc in each of next 4 ch. (5 sc)

Note: Rows 2 through 14 are worked in back loops only.

Row 2: *(Right Side)* Ch 1, turn, sc in each st across. (5 sc)

Row 3: Ch 1, turn, inc in first st, sc in each of next 3 sts, inc in last st. (7 sc)

Row 4: Ch 1, turn, sc in each st across. (7 sc)

Row 5: Ch 1, turn, inc in first st, sc in each of next 5 sts, inc in last st. (9 sc)

Rows 6-10: *(5 rows)* Ch 1, turn, sc in each st across. (9 sc)

Row 11: Ch 1, turn, dec *(using first 2 sts)*, sc in each of next 5 sts, dec *(using last 2 sts)*. (7 sc)

Row 12: Ch 1, turn, sc in each st across. (7 sc)

Row 13: Ch 1, turn, dec *(using first 2 sts)*, sc in each of next 3 sts, dec *(using last 2 sts)*. (5 sc)

Row 14: Ch 1, turn, sc in each st across. (5 sc)

Fasten off, leaving a long tail for sewing. *(image 9)*

1. Use long tail and yarn needle to sew Belly to front of Body, over Rounds 3 to 18. *(image 10)*

TAIL

Round 1: With MC, make a magic ring, 6 sc in ring. (6 sc)

Round 2: Sc in each st around. (6 sc)

Round 3: [Sc in next st, inc in next st] 3 times. (9 sc)

Round 4: Sc in each st around. (9 sc)

Round 5: [Sc in next st, inc in next st, sc in next st] 3 times. (12 sc)

Round 6: Sc in each st around. (12 sc)

Round 7: [Sc in each of next 3 sts, inc in next st] 3 times. (15 sc)

Round 8: Sc in each st around. (15 sc)

Round 9: [Sc in each of next 2 sts, inc in next st, sc in each of next 2 sts] 3 times. (18 sc)

Rounds 10-11: *(2 rounds)* Sc in each st around. (18 sc)

Round 12: [Sc in each of next 5 sts, inc in next st] 3 times. (21 sc)

Rounds 13-15: *(3 rounds)* Sc in each st around. (21 sc)

Round 16: [Sc in each of next 3 sts, inc in next st, sc in each of next 3 sts] 3 times. (24 sc)

Rounds 17-19: *(3 rounds)* Sc in each st around. (24 sc)

Fasten off, leaving a long tail for sewing.

Scales

Note: Use surface crochet along length of Tail to create a row of Scales.

Row 1: With Color B and smaller hook, insert hook under stitch near tip of Tail and pull up a loop, [ch 3, sc in 3rd ch from hook, skip next 2 rounds, sl st under next round] 6 times. (6 Scales) *(image 11)*

Fasten off and weave in ends.

1. Lightly stuff the Tail.

2. Use long tail and yarn needle to sew Tail to back of Body, centered over Rounds 4 to 11. *(images 12 & 13)*

Chloe

About 7½" (19 cm) tall (including Horns)

THE GIRAFFE

MATERIALS & TOOLS

YARN: HELLO Cotton

- **Main Color (MC):** Misty Rose (163) for Face, Arms & Legs
- **Color A:** Mustard (124) for Bodysuit & Hood
- **Color B:** Rusty Brown (167) for Spots
- **Color C:** Dark Brown (127) for Horns & Tail
- **Color D:** Salmon (109) small amount for Cheeks

HOOK SIZE: 2.5 mm hook

OTHER: DMC Embroidery Floss - Black for Eyes and Mouth
Embroidery Needle
Stitch Marker
Yarn Needle
Stuffing
Straight Pins

CHLOE

HEAD

Follow instructions for Basic Doll Head - Front, Back & Head Assembly.

ARMS

Follow instructions for Basic Doll Arm - Make 2.

LEGS & BODY

Follow instructions for Basic Doll Legs only. Refer to images for Basic Doll Body and Joining Arms.

Body

Notes for color changes (Rounds 4 - 12) using chart on page 109 as guide:

a. Change color in the last step of the previous stitch.

b. Drop the non-working yarn to the wrong side, picking it up again for the next color change (stranding the yarn).

Round 1: *(Joining Legs)* With Color A, from Second Leg, ch 3; working on First Leg, sc in next st, sc in each of next 11 sts; working in ch-3, sc in each of next 3 ch; working on Second Leg, sc in each of next 12 sts; working on other side of ch-3, sc in each of next 3 ch. (30 sc)

Round 2: Sc in each of next 6 sts, inc in next st, sc in each of next 14 sts, inc in next st, sc in each of next 8 sts. (32 sc)

Round 3: [Sc in each of next 3 sts, inc in next st] 8 times. (40 sc) Change to Color B.

Round 4: [With Color B, sc in each of next 5 sts; with Color A, sc in each of next 2 sts; with Color B, sc in next st; with Color A, sc in each of next 2 sts] 4 times. (40 sc)

Stuff the Legs.

Round 5: With Color A, sc in next st, [with Color B, sc in each of next 3 sts; with Color A, sc in each of next 2 sts] 7 times; with Color B, sc in each of next 3 sts; with Color A, sc in next st. (40 sc)

Round 6: [With Color A, sc in each of next 2 sts; with Color B, sc in next st; with Color A, sc in each of next 2 sts; with Color B, sc in each of next 5 sts] 4 times. (40 sc)

Round 7: With Color A, sc in each st around. (40 sc) *(image 1)*

Round 8: With Color A, sc in next st; [with Color B, sc in each of next 2 sts; with Color A, sc in each of next 2 sts] 9 times, with Color B; sc in each of next 2 sts; with Color A, sc in next st. (40 sc) *(image 2)*

Round 9: With Color A, sc in next st; with Color B, sc in each of next 2 sts; with Color A, sc in each of next 2 sts; with Color B, sc in each of next 2 sts; with Color A, sc in next st, dec *(using next 2 sts)*; with Color B, sc in next st; [with Color A, sc in each of next 2 sts; with Color B, sc in each of next 2 sts] 4 times; with Color A, sc in next st, dec *(using next 2 sts)*; with Color B, sc in next st; [with Color A, sc in each of next 2 sts; with Color B, sc in each of next 2 sts] 2 times; with Color A, sc in next st. (38 sc)

Round 10: With Color A, sc in each of next 6 sts, dec *(using next 2 sts)*, sc in each of next 21 sts, dec *(using next 2 sts)*, sc in each of next 7 sts. (36 sc)

Round 11: With Color B, sc in each of next 2 sts; with Color A, sc in each of next 2 sts; with Color B, dec *(using next 2 sts)*, sc in next st; with Color A, sc in each of next 2 sts; with Color B, sc in next st; dec *(using next 2 sts)*; with Color A, sc in each of next 2 sts; with Color B, sc in each of next 2 sts; with Color A, dec *(using next 2 sts)*; with Color B, sc in each of next 2 sts; with Color A, sc in each of next 2 sts; with Color B, dec *(using next 2 sts)*, sc in next st; with Color A, sc in each of next 2 sts; with Color B, sc in next st, dec *(using next 2 sts)*; with Color A, sc in each of next 2 sts; with Color B, sc in each of next 2 sts; with Color A, dec *(using next 2 sts)*. (30 sc)

Round 12: With Color A, sc in next st; [with Color B, sc in next st; with Color A, sc in each of next 3 sts] 3 times; with Color B, sc in next st; with Color A, sc in each of next 2 sts; [with Color B, sc in next st; with Color A, sc in each of next 3 sts] 3 times; with Color B, sc in next st; with Color A, sc in next st. (30 sc)

Continue with Color A.

Round 13: Sc in each st around. (30 sc)

Round 14: [Sc in each of next 3 sts, dec] 6 times. (24 sc)

Round 15: Sc in each st around. (24 sc)

Start stuffing Body.

Round 16: [Sc in each of next 4 sts, dec] 4 times. (20 sc)

Note: *When attaching each Arm, flatten the top of the Arm and hold against the Body with the decrease stitches on Arm Round 5 facing outwards. Work the "attaching" stitches through both the layers of the Arm and the Body together.*

Round 17: *(Attaching Arms)* Sc in each of next 4 sts; working on First Arm & Body, sc in each of next 4 sts *(First Arm attached)*; working on Body only, sc in each of next 8 sts; working on Second Arm & Body, sc in each of next 4 sts *(Second Arm attached)*. (20 sc)

Round 18: Sc in each of next 4 sts, [dec] 2 times, sc in each of next 8 sts, [dec] 2 times. (16 sc)

Round 19: *(Neck)* Sc in each st around. (16 sc)

Fasten off, leaving a long tail for sewing.

DOLL ASSEMBLY

Follow Basic Doll Assembly Instructions.

HOOD

Follow instructions for Basic Hood.

SPOTS

Small (Make 3)

Round 1: With Color B, make a magic ring, 6 sc in ring; join with sl st to first sc. (6 sc)

Fasten off, leaving a long tail for sewing.

Large (Make 1)

Round 1: With Color B, make a magic ring, ch 2, 8 hdc in magic ring; join with sl st to first hdc. (8 hdc)

Fasten off, leaving a long tail for sewing.

1. Use long tails and yarn needle to sew Spots to front of Hood. *(image 3)*

HORN (Make 2)

Round 1: With Color C, make a magic ring, 6 sc in ring. (6 sc)

Round 2: Inc in each st around. (12 sc)

Round 3: Sc in each st around. (12 sc)

Change to Color A.

Round 4: [Sc in each of next 2 sts, dec] 3 times. (9 sc)

Round 5: [Sc in next st, dec] 3 times. (6 sc)

Rounds 6-8: *(3 rounds)* Sc in each st around. (6 sc)

Fasten off, leaving a long tail for sewing.

1. Stuff Horns.

2. Position Horns on top of Head, just behind the Hoodline with about 2-3 stitches between them, and using long tail and yarn needle, sew in place. *(images 4 & 5)*

EAR (Make 2)

Round 1: With Color A, starting with a long tail, ch 8; sl st in 2nd ch from hook, sc in next ch, dc in each of next 4 ch, 4 hdc in last ch; working on other side of starting ch *(image 6)*, dc in each of next 4 chs, sc in next ch, sl st in last ch. (16 sts) *(image 7)*

Round 2: Ch 1, sl st in each st around. (16 sl sts)

Fasten off and weave in end.

1. Position Ears on top of Head, just behind the Hoodline and about 3-4 stitches away from each Horn, and using starting tail and yarn needle, sew in place. *(image 8)*

FACE - use photos as guide

TIP: *Use straight pins to mark positions of facial features, based on preferred placement. (image 9)*

1. With Black Floss (using 4 to 6 strands, depending on preferred thickness), embroider Mouth over Round 8 on Face.

2. For Eyes, create arcs about 3-4 rounds wide and 2-3 stitches tall. *(image 10)*

3. Use 2 strands of Floss to embroider eyebrows.

4. With Color D, embroider a few short, straight stitches under the outer edge of each Eye for Cheeks. *(image 11)*

TAIL

With Color A, ch 6.

Fasten off, leaving a yarn tail for sewing.

1. Use yarn needle to sew Tail to back of Body, between Rounds 7 & 8.

2. With Color C, knot several short strands of yarn to the last chain stitch.

3. Fray the yarn ends, and trim the Tail. *(image 12)*

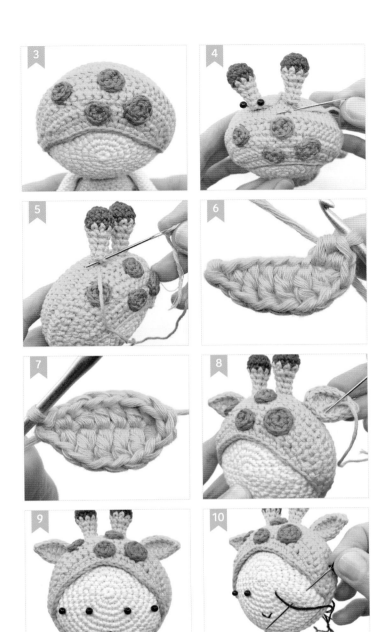

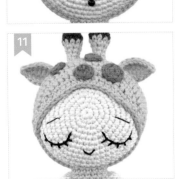

Body Colour Chart

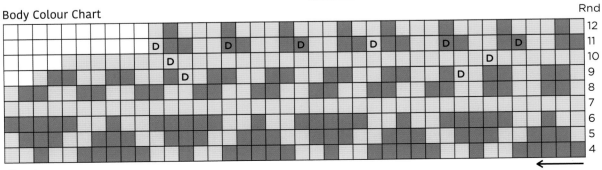

D = decrease

109

Olivia

About 7" (18 cm) tall (including Mane)

THE LION

MATERIALS & TOOLS

YARN: HELLO Cotton

- **Main Color (MC):** Misty Rose (163) for Face, Arms & Legs
- **Color A:** Tobacco (166) for Bodysuit & Hood
- **Color B:** Dark Brown (127) for Paw Embroidery, Muzzle & Mane
- **Color C:** Dark Beige (158) - for Ears & Embroidery
- **Color D:** Salmon (109) - small amount for Cheeks

HOOK SIZE: 2.5 mm hook

OTHER: DMC Embroidery Floss
Black for Eyes and Mouth

Embroidery Needle

Stitch Marker

Yarn Needle

Stuffing

Straight Pins

HEAD

Follow instructions for Basic Doll Head - Front, Back & Head Assembly.

ARMS

Follow instructions for Basic Doll Arm - Make 2.

LEGS & BODY

First Leg

Round 1: *(Paw)* With Color A, make a magic ring, 6 sc in ring. (6 sc)

Round 2: Inc in each st around. (12 sc)

Rounds 3-4: *(2 rounds)* Sc in each st around. (12 sc)

Change to MC.

Round 5: Working in back loops only, sc in each st around. (12 sc)

Rounds 6-12: *(7 rounds)* Sc in each st around. (12 sc)

Fasten off.

Second Leg

Rounds 1-12: *(12 rounds)* Repeat Rounds 1-12 of First Leg. Sc in each of next 6 sc *(to move end of round position)*.

Change to Color A.

Body

Rounds 1-19: Follow Basic Doll Body Rounds 1-19.

Fasten off, leaving a long tail for sewing.

1. With Color B and yarn needle, make 3 vertical straight stitches on front of each Paw, over Rounds 2 and 3. *(image 1)*

2. With Color C and yarn needle, make a series of short, straight stitches across front of Body, between Rounds 9 and 17, in a rough zig-zag pattern. *(image 2)*

DOLL ASSEMBLY

Follow Basic Doll Assembly Instructions.

HOOD

Follow instructions for Basic Hood.

FACE - use photos as guide

TIP: Use straight pins to mark positions of facial features, based on preferred placement.

1. With Black Floss (using 4 to 6 strands, depending on preferred thickness), embroider Mouth over Round 8 on Face.

2. For Eyes, create arcs about 3-4 rounds wide and 2-3 stitches tall.

3. Use 2 strands of Floss to embroider eyebrows.

4. With Color D, embroider a few short, straight stitches under the outer edge of each Eye for Cheeks.

MUZZLE

Round 1: With Color B, make a magic ring, 6 sc in ring. (6 sc)

Round 2: [Sc in next st, inc in next st] 3 times. (9 sc)

Round 3: [Sc in each of next 2 sts, inc in next st] 3 times. (12 sc)

Change to Color A.

Round 4: Sc in each st around. (12 sc)

Round 5: Dec *(using next 2 sts)*, sc in each of next 10 sts. (11 sc)

Rounds 6-11: *(6 rounds)* Sc in each st around. (11 sc)

Joining Row: Flatten Muzzle, skip first st, working through both sides *(to close opening)*, sc in each of next 5 sts.

Fasten off, leaving a long tail for sewing.

1. With Color C and yarn needle, make a series of short, straight stitches across front of Muzzle, between Rounds 6 and 10, in a rough zig-zag pattern. *(image 3)*

2. Use long tail to sew Muzzle to Hood, using pictures as a guide. *(images 4 & 5)*

MANE

Note: Surface Single Crochets are used as a foundation for the Mane.

Notes for Color Changes (Tapestry Crochet Technique) - Mane Row

a. *Change color in the last step of the previous stitch.*

b. *Carry the unused color by working over it until the next color change (no stranding visible).*

Foundation Row: With Color A, attach yarn around first stitch next to Neck, between final round of Back of Head and the Hoodline *(image 6)*; ch 1, surface sc in each of next 58 sts across Head *(ending at Neck on other side of Body)* *(images 7 & 8)*. (58 sc)

Fasten off and weave in ends.

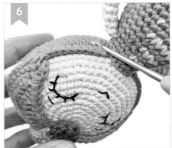

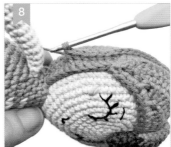

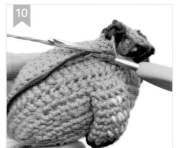

Mane Row: Attach Color A to first st of Foundation Row, ch 3 (*counts as first dc, now and throughout*) *(image 9)*, 2 dc in same st, 3 dc in next st; [with Color B, 3 dc in each of next 2 sts; with Color A, 3 dc in each of next 2 sts] 14 times. (174 dc) *(image 10)*

Fasten off and weave in ends.

EAR (Make 2)

Note: *Ears are worked in rows, starting with a magic ring.*

Row 1: *(Right Side)* With Color C, make a magic ring, 6 sc in ring. (6 sc) Tighten ring but do not join round.

Row 2: Ch 1, turn, sc in first st, inc in each of next 4 sts, sc in last st. (10 sc) Change to Color A.

Row 3: Ch 1, turn, sc in first st, sc in each of next 2 sts, hdc in each of next 4 sts, sc in each of next 3 sts. (6 sc & 4 hdc)

Fasten off, leaving a long tail for sewing.

1. Use long tail and yarn needle to sew Ears to Hoodline (in front of Mane) about 4 to 5 stitches from either side of Muzzle *(image 11)*.

TAIL

With Color A, ch 20, sl st in 2ⁿᵈ ch from hook, sl st in each of next 18 ch. (19 sl sts)

Fasten off, leaving a yarn tail for sewing.

1. Use yarn needle to sew Tail to center back of Body, between Rounds 8 & 9.

2. With Color C, knot several short strands of yarn to the last chain stitch.

3. Fray the yarn ends, and trim the Tail. *(image 12)*

Myrtle

The Bee

About 6¾" (17 cm) tall

MATERIALS & TOOLS

YARN: HELLO Cotton

    Main color (MC): Misty Rose (163) - for Face, Arms & Legs

    Color A: Yellow (123) - for Bodysuit

    Color B: Black (160) - for Bodysuit, Hood, Antenna & Stinger

    Color C: White (154) - for Wings

    Color D: Dark Salmon (112) - for Cheeks

HOOK SIZE: 2.5 mm hook

OTHER: DMC Embroidery Floss - Black for Eyes and Mouth

    Embroidery Needle

    Stitch Marker

    Yarn Needle

    Stuffing

    Straight Pins

SPECIAL STITCHES & TECHNIQUES

Single Crochet Spike Stitch (sc-sp)

Insert hook in specified stitch one round below current round, pull up loop to height of stitches in current round, yarn over and draw through both loops on hook. (single crochet spike stitch made)

MYRTLE

HEAD

Front (Face)

Round 1: With MC, make a magic ring, 6 sc in ring. (6 sc)

Round 2: Inc in each st around. (12 sc)

Round 3: [Sc in next st, inc in next st] 6 times. (18 sc)

Round 4: [Sc in next st, inc in next st, sc in next st] 6 times. (24 sc)

Round 5: [Sc in each of next 3 sts, inc in next st] 6 times. (30 sc)

Round 6: [Sc in each of next 2 sts, inc in next st, sc in each of next 2 sts] 6 times. (36 sc)

Round 7: [Sc in each of next 5 sts, inc in next st] 6 times. (42 sc)

Round 8: [Sc in each of next 3 sts, inc in next st, sc in each of next 3 sts] 6 times. (48 sc)

Round 9: [Sc in each of next 7 sts, inc in next st] 6 times. (54 sc)

Round 10: [Sc in each of next 4 sts, inc in next st, sc in each of next 4 sts] 6 times. (60 sc)

Round 11: [Sc in each of next 9 sts, inc in next st] 6 times. (66 sc)

Rounds 12-13: Sc in each st around. (66 sc)

Fasten off.

Back (Hood)

Round 1: With Color A, make a magic ring, 6 sc in ring. (6 sc)

Change to Color B

Round 2: Inc in each st around. (12 sc)

Round 3: [Sc in next st, inc in next st] 6 times. (18 sc)

Change to Color A

Round 4: [Sc in next st, inc in next st, sc in next st] 6 times. (24 sc)

Round 5: [Sc in each of next 3 sts, inc in next st] 6 times. (30 sc)

Round 6: [Sc in each of next 2 sts, inc in next st, sc in each of next 2 sts] 6 times. (36 sc)

Change to Color B

Round 7: [Sc in each of next 5 sts, inc in next st] 6 times. (42 sc)

Round 8: [Sc in each of next 3 sts, inc in next st, sc in

each of next 3 sts] 6 times. (48 sc)

Change to Color A

Round 9: [Sc in each of next 7 sts, inc in next st] 6 times. (54 sc)

Round 10: [Sc in each of next 4 sts, inc in next st, sc in each of next 4 sts] 6 times. (60 sc)

Round 11: [Sc in each of next 9 sts, inc in next st] 6 times. (66 sc)

Change to Color B

Rounds 12-13: *(2 Rounds)* Sc in each st around. (66 sc) Do not fasten off. Continue with Head Assembly.

Head Assembly

1. Hold the Front and Back together with right sides facing outwards, and Front of Head facing you. *(image 1)*

2. With Color B, insert hook in both the next stitch on Front and corresponding stitch on Back *(image 2)* and work a single crochet stitch. This is the first stitch of the "Hoodline".

3. Working through both Front & Back together, single crochet in each of next 65 stitches to complete the Hoodline (66 stitches) *(image 3)*, stuffing Head firmly before finishing the round. *(image 4)*

4. Join the round with a slip stitch in the first single crochet stitch.

5. Fasten off and weave in ends. *(image 5)*

6. Set Head aside.

ARMS

Round 1: With MC, make a magic ring, 6 sc in ring. (6 sc)

Round 2: Inc in each st around. (12 sc)

Rounds 3-4: *(2 rounds)* Sc in each st around. (12 sc)

Round 5: Sc in each of next 6 sts, [dec] 3 times. (9 sc)

Rounds 6-14: *(9 rounds)* Sc in each st around. (9 sc)

Round 15: Dec, sc in each of next 7 sts. (8 sc) Sc in each of next 3 sts *(to position decreases on outer Arm)*.

Fasten off.

LEGS & BODY

First Leg

Round 1: With MC, make a magic ring, 6 sc in ring. (6 sc)

Round 2: Inc in each st around. (12 sc)

Rounds 3-12: *(10 rounds)* Sc in each st around. (12 sc)

Fasten off.

Second Leg

Rounds 1-12: *(12 rounds)* With MC, repeat Rounds 1-12 of First Leg.

Change to Color A. Continue with Body.

Body

Round 1: *(Joining Legs)* From Second Leg *(with Color A)*, ch 3; working on First Leg, sc in next st, sc in each of next 11 sts; working in ch-3, sc in each of next 3 ch; working on Second Leg, sc in each of next 12 sts; working on other side of ch-3, sc in each of next 3 ch. (30 sc)

Round 2: Sc in each of next 6 sts, inc in next st, sc in each of next 14 sts, inc in next st, sc in each of next 8 sts. (32 sc)

Round 3: [Sc in each of next 3 sts, inc in next st] 8 times. (40 sc)

Change to Color B.

Stuff the Legs.

Rounds 4-5: *(2 rounds)* Sc in each st around. (40 sc)

Change to Color A.

Rounds 6-8: *(3 rounds)* Sc in each st around. (40 sc)

Change to Color B.

Round 9: Sc in each of next 8 sts, dec, sc in each of next 18 sts, dec, sc in each of next 10 sts. (38 sc)

Round 10: Sc in each of next 8 sts, dec, sc in each of next 17 sts, dec, sc in each of next 9 sts. (36 sc)

Change to Color A.

Round 11: [Sc in each of next 4 sts, dec] 6 times. (30 sc)

Rounds 12-13: *(2 rounds)* Sc in each st around. (30 sc)

Change to Color B.

Round 14: [Sc in each of next 3 sts, dec] 6 times. (24 sc)

Round 15: Sc in each st around. (24 sc)

Change to Color A.

Start stuffing Body.

Round 16: [Sc in each of next 4 sts, dec] 4 times. (20 sc)

Note: *When attaching each Arm, flatten the top of the Arm and hold against the Body with the decrease stitches on Arm Round 5 facing outwards. Work the "attaching" stitches through both the layers of the Arm and the Body together.*

Round 17: *(Attaching Arms)* Sc in each of next 4 sts; working on First Arm & Body, sc in each of next 4 sts *(First Arm attached)*; working on Body only, sc in each of next 8 sts; working on Second Arm & Body, sc in each of next 4 sts *(Second Arm attached)*. (20 sc)

Round 18: Sc in each of next 4 sts, [dec] 2 times, sc in each of next 8 sts, [dec] 2 times. (16 sc)

Change to Color B.

Round 19: *(Neck)* Sc in each st around. (16 sc) *(image 6)*

Fasten off, leaving a long tail for sewing.

DOLL ASSEMBLY

1. Finish stuffing the Body.

2. Using long tail and yarn needle, sew Body to Head, working through all 16 sts around Neck. *(images 7 & 8)*

TIP: *Maintain a wide, round Neck opening, adding extra stuffing before finishing.*

HOOD

Row 1: *(Wrong Side)* With Color B, ch 36, sc in 2nd ch from hook, sc in each of next 34 ch. (35 sc)

Row 2: *(Right Side)* Ch 1, turn, skip first st, dec *(using next 2 sts)*, [sc in each of next 4 sts, dec, sc in each of next 4 sts] 3 times, dec *(using last 2 sts)*. (29 sc)

Row 3: Ch 1, turn, skip first st, dec, sc in each of next 24 sts, dec. (26 sc)

Row 4: Ch 1, turn, skip first st, dec, sc in each of next 3 sts, [dec, sc in each of next 5 sts] 2 times, dec, sc in each of next 2 sts, dec. (20 sc)

Row 5: Ch 1, turn, skip first st, dec, sc in each of next 15 sts, dec. (17 sc)

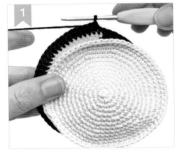

Row 6: Ch 1, turn, skip first st, sc in each of next 3 sts, [dec, sc in each of next 2 sts] 3 times, sl st into last st. (13 sts)

Fasten off and weave in ends. *(image 9)*

Edging: With right side facing, attach Color B to end of Row 1; ch 2 *(counts as first hdc)*, working in sides of rows, hdc in same Row 1, hdc in each of next 5 rows; working across Row 6, sc-sp in first st, sc in each of the next 11 sts *(image 10)*, sc-sp in last st; working in sides of rows, hdc in each of next 5 row, 2 hdc in Row 1. (14 hdc, 11 sc, & 2 sc-sp)

Fasten off, leaving a long tail for sewing. *(image 11)*

1. Position the Hood, centered at top of Head. Gently stretch the Hood to fit around face, and pin in place. *(image 12)*

2. Use long tail and yarn needle to whipstitch the starting chain of Hood to Hoodline.

FACE - use photos as guide

TIP: *Use straight pins to mark positions of facial features, based on preferred placement.*

1. With Black Floss (using 4 to 6 strands, depending on preferred thickness), embroider Mouth over Round 8 on Face.

2. For Eyes, embroider several vertical straight stitches (over 2 stitches each). *(image 13)*

3. Use 2 strands of Floss to add eyelashes and eyebrows.

Cheek (Make 2)

Row 1: With Color D, make a magic ring, ch 3, 9 dc in ring. (9 dc) Tighten ring but do not join round, shaping cheeks as half-circles. *(image 14)*

Fasten off, leaving a long tail for sewing.

1. Position Cheeks just below the end of the Hood, with the straight edge along the Hoodline. *(image 15)*

2. Use long tails and yarn needle to sew Cheeks in place.

ANTENNA (Make 2)

Row 1: With Color B, ch 12; working in back bumps of chain stitches, hdc in 2nd ch from hook, sl st in each of next 10 ch. (1 hdc & 10 sl sts)

Fasten off, leaving a long tail for sewing.

1. Sew Antennae to top of Head, just behind Hoodline, with about 8 stitches between them. *(image 16)*

WING (Make 2)

Round 1: With Color C, make a magic ring, 6 sc in ring. (6 sc)

Round 2: Inc in each st around. (12 sc)

Round 3: Sc in each st around. (12 sc)

Round 4: [Sc in next st, inc in next st] 6 times. (18 sc)

Rounds 5-7: *(3 rounds)* Sc in each st around. (18 sc)

Round 8: [Sc in next st, dec] 6 times. (12 sc)

Rounds 9-10: *(2 rounds)* Sc in each st around. (12 sc)

Round 11: [Sc in each of next 2 sts, dec] 3 times. (9 sc)

Rounds 12-15: *(4 rounds)* Sc in each st around. (9 sc)

Fasten off, leaving a long tail for sewing.

Wing Detail - use photos as guide

1. Flatten Wings and embroider Wing Veins, using a single strand of Black Floss. Start by making a rough outline around one side of Wing, then add a random pattern of geometric shapes within outline, using straight stitches.

2. Repeat on other side of Wing.

3. Repeat steps 1 & 2 on second Wing. *(image 17)*

4. Using long tails and yarn needle, sew Wings to back of Body (between Arms) over Rounds 14 to 17. *(image 18)*

STINGER

Round 1: With Color B, make a magic ring, 5 sc in ring. (5 sc)

Round 2: Sc in each of next 2 sts, inc in next st, sc in each of next 2 sts. (6 sc)

Round 3: Sc in each st around. (6 sc)

Round 4: [Inc in next st, sc in next st] 3 times. (9 sc)

Round 5: Sc in each st around. (9 sc)

Fasten off, leaving a long tail for sewing.

1. Flatten Stinger and use yarn needle to sew to center back of Body, over Round 5. *(images 19 & 20)*

World Dolls

Follow instructions for chosen World Doll, referring to Basic Doll instructions when needed.

Ireland · Argentina · Turkiye

Germany · Uzbekistan · Spain

About 7½" (19 cm) tall

SPECIAL STITCHES & TECHNIQUES

Double Crochet Decrease (dc-dec)

Yarn over and insert hook in stitch or space specified, pull up a loop (3 loops on hook), yarn over and draw through two loops on hook (2 loops remain on hook); yarn over, insert hook in next stitch or space and pull up a loop (4 loops on hook), yarn over and draw through two loops on hook (3 loops remain on hook). Yarn over and draw through all three loops on hook. (double crochet decrease made)

Half Treble Crochet (htr)

Yarn over twice and insert hook in stitch or space specified, pull up a loop (4 loops on hook); yarn over, draw through 2 loops on hook, yarn over and draw through remaining 3 loops on hook. (half-treble made)

BASIC DOLL

HEAD

Front (Face)

Round 1: With MC, make a magic ring, 6 sc in ring. (6 sc)

Round 2: Inc in each st around. (12 sc)

Round 3: [Sc in next st, inc in next st] 6 times. (18 sc)

Round 4: [Sc in next st, inc in next st, sc in next st] 6 times. (24 sc)

Round 5: [Sc in each of next 3 sts, inc in next st] 6 times. (30 sc)

Round 6: [Sc in each of next 2 sts, inc in next st, sc in each of next 2 sts] 6 times. (36 sc)

Round 7: [Sc in each of next 5 sts, inc in next st] 6 times. (42 sc)

Round 8: [Sc in each of next 3 sts, inc in next st, sc in each of next 3 sts] 6 times. (48 sc)

Round 9: [Sc in each of next 7 sts, inc in next st] 6 times. (54 sc)

Round 10: [Sc in each of next 4 sts, inc in next st, sc in each of next 4 sts] 6 times. (60 sc)

Round 11: [Sc in each of next 9 sts, inc in next st] 6 times. (66 sc)

Rounds 12-13: *(2 rounds)* Sc in each st around. (66 sc)

Fasten off.

Back (Hair)

Rounds 1-12: *(12 Rounds)* With Color A, repeat Rounds 1-12 of Head Front (omitting last round). Do not fasten off.

Head Assembly

1. Hold the Front and Back together with right sides facing outwards. *(image 1)*

2. With Color A, single crochet in both the next stitch on Back (and corresponding stitch on Front). This is the first stitch of the "Hairline". *(image 2)*

3. Working through both Back & Front together, single crochet in each of next {number for specific Doll} stitches, to complete the Hairline. *(image 3)*

4. Change to MC, and continue working single crochet stitches *(image 4)*, stuffing the Head firmly before finishing the round. *(image 5)*

5. Join the round with a slip stitch in the first single crochet stitch.

6. Fasten off and weave in ends. *(image 6)*

7. Set Head aside.

ARM (Make 2)

Round 1: With MC, make a magic ring, 6 sc in ring. (6 sc)

Round 2: [Inc in next st, sc in each of next 2 sts] 2 times. (8 sc)

Rounds 3-15: *(13 rounds)* Sc in each st around. (8 sc)

Fasten off.

1. Stuff the lower half of each Arm, leaving the remainder of Arm unstuffed.

2. Set Arms aside.

BODY

Base

Round 1: With Color B, make a magic ring, 6 sc in ring. (6 sc)

Round 2: [Sc in next st, inc in next st] 3 times. (9 sc)

Round 3: Sc in each st around. (9 sc)

Round 4: [Sc in next st, inc in next st, sc in next st] 3 times. (12 sc)

Round 5: Sc in each st around. (12 sc)

Round 6: [Sc in each of next 3 sts, inc in next st] 3 times. (15 sc)

Round 7: [Sc in each of next 2 sts, inc in next st, sc in each of next 2 sts] 3 times. (18 sc)

Round 8: [Sc in each of next 5 sts, inc in next st] 3 times. (21 sc)

Round 9: [Sc in each of next 3 sts, inc in next st, sc in each of next 3 sts] 3 times. (24 sc)

Dress

Round 10: Working in back loops only, sc in each st around. (24 sc)

Round 11: Sc in each st around. (24 sc)

Round 12: Sc in each of next 2 sts, inc in next st, sc in each of next 12 sts, inc in next st, sc in each of next 8 sts. (26 sc)

Rounds 13-16: *(4 rounds)* Sc in each st around. (26 sc)

Round 17: Sc in each of next 3 sts, inc in next st, sc in each of next 13 sts, inc in next st, sc in each of next 8 sts. (28 sc)

Rounds 18-21: *(4 rounds)* Sc in each st around. (28 sc)

Round 22: Sc in each of next 5 sts, inc in next st, sc in each of next 14 sts, inc in next st, sc in each of next 7 sts. (30 sc)

Rounds 23-26: *(4 rounds)* Sc in each st around. (30 sc) *(image 7)*

1. Invert the first 9 rounds up inside Dress, leaving the unused loops of Round 9 around base of Dress. *(images 8 & 9)* This inverted Base assists the Doll to stand unaided.

2. Start stuffing the Body, adding stuffing evenly around the Base, making sure the inverted rounds stay inside the Dress.

Round 27: [Sc in each of next 5 sts, inc in next st] 5 times. (35 sc)

Rounds 28-31: *(4 rounds)* Sc in each st around. (35 sc)

Round 32: [Sc in each each of next 3 sts, dec] 7 times. (28 sc)

Rounds 33-35: *(3 rounds)* Sc in each st around. (28 sc)

Round 36: Sc in each of next 8 sts, dec, sc in each of next 12 sts, dec, sc in each of next 4 sts. (26 sc)

Round 37: Sc in each of next 8 sts, dec, sc in each of next 11 sts, dec, sc in each of next 3 sts. (24 sc)

Round 38: [Sc in each of next 2 sts, dec] 6 times. (18 sc)

Note: *When attaching each Arm, flatten the top of the Arm and hold against the Body. Work the "attaching" stitches through both the layers of the Arm and the Body together.*

Round 39: *(Attaching Arms)* Sc in each of next 4 sts on Body; working on First Arm & Body, sc in each of next 4 sts *(image 10)* *(First Arm attached)*; working on Body only, sc in each of next 6 sts *(image 11)*; working on Second Arm & Body, sc in each of next 4 sts *(Second Arm attached)*. (18 sc)

Round 40: Sc in each of next 5 sts, dec, sc in each of next 8 sts, dec, sc in next st. (16 sc)

Round 41: *(Neck)* Sc in each st around. (16 sc)

Fasten off, leaving a long tail for sewing.

Base Trim

Holding Dress upside down, attach Color B at back of Dress to first unworked front loop on Round 9. *(image 12)*

Round 1: Working in unused front loops, sl st in each st around. (24 sl sts) *(image 13)*

Fasten off and weave in ends.

DOLL ASSEMBLY

1. Finish stuffing the Body.

2. Using long tail from Body and yarn needle, sew Body to Head, working through all 16 stitches around Neck. *(images 14 & 15)*

TIP: *Ensure Body is centered between ends of Hairline. Maintain a wide, round Neck opening, adding extra stuffing before finishing.*

BASIC FACE - use photos as guide

TIP: Use straight pins to mark positions of facial features, based on preferred placement.

1. With Black Floss (using 4 to 6 strands, depending on preferred thickness), embroider Mouth over Round 9 on Face.

2. For Eyes, create arcs about 3-4 rounds wide and 2-3 stitches tall. Use 2 strands of Floss to embroider eyebrows.

3. With Cheek Color, embroider a few short, straight stitches under the outer edge of each Eye.

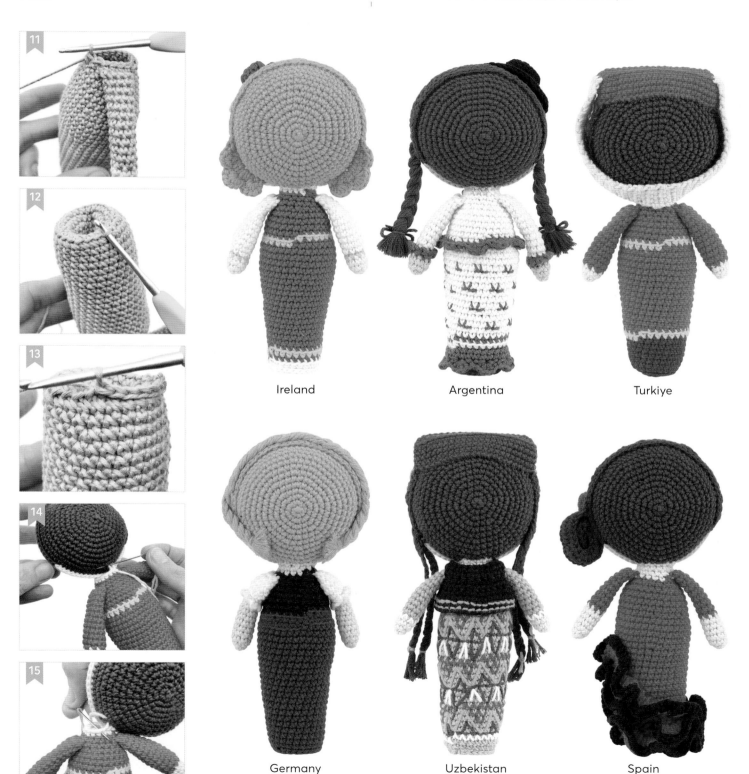

Ireland   Argentina   Turkiye

Germany   Uzbekistan   Spain

Maeve

IRELAND

Maeve in her traditional green dress.

MATERIALS & TOOLS

YARN: HELLO Cotton

- **Main Color (MC):** Seashell (161) for Face & Arms
- **Color A:** Orange (119) for Hair
- **Color B:** White (154) - for Dress (contrast)
- **Color C:** Kelly Green (132) for Dress (main) and Three-Leaf Clover
- **Color D:** Yellow (123) for Dress (trim) and Headband
- Small amount of: Salmon (109) for Cheeks

HOOK SIZE: 2.5 mm hook
2.0 mm hook for Three-Leaf Clover

OTHER: DMC Embroidery Floss - Black for Eyes and Mouth
Embroidery Needle
Stitch Marker
Yarn Needle
Stuffing
Straight Pins

HEAD

Follow instructions for Basic Doll Head - Front & Back.

Head Assembly

Follow Steps 1-7 of Basic Doll Head Assembly, and in Step 3, single crochet in each of next 54 stitches to complete the Hairline. (55 stitches)

ARM (Make 2)

Rounds 1-3: Follow instructions for Basic Doll Arm Rounds 1-3.

Change to Color D.

Round 4: Sc in each st around. (8 sc)

Change to Color B

Round 5: [Sc in next st, inc in next st] 4 times. (12 sc)

Rounds 6-11: *(6 rounds)* Sc in each st around. (12 sc)

Round 12: [Sc in next st, dec] 4 times. (8 sc)

Rounds 13-15: *(3 rounds)* Sc in each st around. (8 sc)

Fasten off.

1. Stuff the lower half of each Arm, leaving the remainder of Arm unstuffed.

2. Set Arms aside.

BODY

Notes for Color Changes from Round 11 onwards:

a. *Change color in the last step of the previous stitch.*

b. *Drop the non-working yarn to the wrong side, picking it up again for the next color change (stranding the yarn). Alternatively, cut and tie yarn ends on inside of Dress.*

Rounds 1-10: Follow instructions for Basic Doll Body Base & Dress Rounds 1-10.

Change to Color C.

Round 11: Working in back loops only, sc in each of next 6 sts; with Color B, working through both loops, sc in each of next 4 sts; with Color C, working in back loops only, sc in each of next 14 sts. (24 sc)

Round 12: With Color D, sc in each of next 2 sts, inc in next st, sc in each of next 4 sts; with Color B, sc in each of next 3 sts; with Color D, sc in each of next 5 sts, inc in next st, sc in each of next 8 sts. (26 sc)

Round 13: With Color C, working in back loops only, sc in each of next 8 sts; with Color B, working through both loops, sc in each of next 3 sts; with Color C, working in back loops only, sc in each of next 15 sts. (26 sc)

Rounds 14-15: *(2 rounds)* Sc in each of next 8 sts; with Color B, sc in each of next 3 sts; with Color C, sc in each of next 15 sts. (26 sc)

Round 16: Sc in each of next 9 sts; with Color B, sc in each of next 2 sts; with Color C, sc in each of next 15 sts. (26 sc)

Round 17: Sc in each of next 3 sts, inc in next st, sc in each of next 5 sts; with Color B, sc in each of next 2 sts; with Color C, sc in each of next 6 sts, inc in next st, sc in each of next 8 sts. (28 sc)

Rounds 18-19: *(2 rounds)* Sc in each of next 11 sts; with Color B, sc in next st; with Color C, sc in each of next 16 sts. (28 sc) *(image 1)*

Continue in Color C.

Rounds 20-31: *(12 rounds)* Follow instructions for Basic Doll Body Rounds 20-31.

Change to Color D.

Round 32: [Sc in each each of next 3 sts, dec] 7 times. (28 sc)

Change to Color C.

Round 33: Working in back loops only, sc in each st around. (28 sc)

Rounds 34-35: *(2 rounds)* Sc in each st around. (28 sc)

Round 36: Sc in each of next 8 sts, dec, sc in each of next 12 sts, dec, sc in each of next 4 sts. (26 sc)

Round 37: Sc in each of next 8 sts, dec, sc in each of next 2 sts; with Color B, working in back loops only, sc in each of next 5 sts; with Color C, sc in each of next 4 sts, dec, sc in each of next 3 sts. (24 sc)

Round 38: [Dec, sc in each of next 2 sts] 2 times, dec, sc in next st; with Color B, sc in next st, dec, sc in each of next 2 sts; with Color C, [dec, sc in each of next 2 sts] 2 times. (18 sc)

Note: When attaching each Arm, flatten the top of the Arm and hold against the Body. Work the "attaching" stitches through both the layers of the Arm and the Body together.

Round 39: *(Attaching Arms)* Sc in each of next 3 sts on Body; working on First Arm & Body, sc in each of next 4 sts *(First Arm attached)*; working on Body only, sc in next st; with MC, sc in next st; working in back loops only, sc in each of next 3 sts; with Color C, sc in next st; working on Second Arm & Body, sc in each of next 4 sts *(Second Arm attached)*, sc in next st. (18 sc)

Round 40: Sc in each of next 4 sts, dec, sc in each of next 2 sts; with MC, sc in each of next 4 sts; with Color C, sc in each of next 2 sts, dec, sc in each of next 2 sts. (16 sc)

Round 41: *(Neck)* With MC, working in back loops only, sc in each of next 7 sts; working in both loops, sc in each of next 4 sts; working in back loops only, sc in each of next 5 sts. (16 sc)

Fasten off, leaving a long tail for sewing. *(image 2)*

Base Trim: Follow instructions for Basic Doll Body Base Trim.

DOLL ASSEMBLY

Follow Basic Doll Assembly Instructions.

DRESS DETAILS - use photos as guide

1. With Color C and yarn needle, make a few small vertical straight stitches at the Neckline of the Dress, to neaten color changes. *(image 3)*

2. With Color D, embroider two long vertical stitches down front of Dress - one from top of Round 36 to the Belt (Round 32), and the other from the Belt to top of triangular panel (in Color B) of Dress (Round 19). Embroider a long stitch on either side of the triangular panel, between Rounds 12 and 19. *(image 4)*

3. With Color B and yarn needle, wrap yarn evenly around the long stitches made in step 2, catching small amounts of the crochet stitches on the Dress, to keep the straight stitches in position. *(image 5)*

HAIR

Hair Bangs

Note: The Hair Bangs are worked as a single piece in rows, starting with a magic ring.

Row 1: *(Right Side)* With Color A, make a magic ring, ch 3 *(counts as first dc, now and throughout)*, 5 dc in ring. (6 dc) Tighten ring but do not join round.

Row 2: Ch 3, turn, dc in first st, 2 dc in each of next 4 sts, 2 dc in last st *(3rd ch of ch-3)*. (12 dc)

Row 3: Ch 3, turn, dc in first st, [dc in next st, 2 dc in next st] 5 times, dc in last st. (18 dc)

Row 4: Ch 3, turn, 2 dc in next st, [dc in each of next 2 sts, 2 dc in next st] 5 times, dc in last st. (24 dc)

Row 5: Ch 2 *(counts as first hdc, now and throughout)*, turn, hdc in each of next 22 sts, hdc in last st. (24 hdc)

Row 6: Ch 3, turn, dc in each of next 11 sts. (12 dc) Leave remaining sts unworked.

Row 7: Ch 2, turn, dc in each of next 5 sts, htr in each of next 3 sts, tr in each of next 2 sts, tr in last st. (1 hdc, 5 dc, 3 htr & 3 tr)

Fasten off and weave in ends.

Row 6a: With right side facing, attach Color A to first st on Row 5 *(2nd ch of ch-2)*, ch 3 *(image 6)*, dc in each of next 11 sts. (12 dc)

Row 7a: Ch 2, turn, dc in each of next 5 sts, htr in each of next 3 sts, tr in each of next 2 sts, tr in last st. (1 hdc, 5 dc, 3 htr & 3 tr)

Fasten off, leaving a long tail for sewing. *(image 7)*

1. Position Hair Bangs on Head Front, aligned with the Hairline. Gently shape to fit, leaving eight (8) Hairline stitches open on either side of Hair Bangs. *(image 8)*

2. Use long tail and yarn needle to sew Hair Bangs in place, along the Hairline. *(image 9)*

Hair Curl

Note: The Hair Curls are worked in the open 8 stitches on Hairline. There are no turning chains in the rows.

Attach Color A to first open stitch on Hairline, below Hair Bangs. *(image 10)*

Row 1: Sc in next st, 2 hdc in next st, 3 hdc in each of next 2 sts, 2 hdc in next st, sc in next st, sl st in last st. (2 sc, 10 hdc & 1 sl st) *(image 11)*

Row 2: Turn, skip first sl st, [5 hdc in next st, skip next st, sl st in next st, skip next st] 2 times, 3 hdc in next st, skip next st, sl st in next st, sl st in same st as joining. (3 "Curls") *(image 12)*

Fasten off and weave in ends.

Repeat Hair Curl on other side of Head. *(image 13)*

FACE - use photos as guide

1. Follow Basic Doll Face Instructions.

2. Split a length of Color A, and embroider Freckles, using several small straight stitches below each eye. *(image 14)*

HEADBAND

Row 1: With Color D, ch 31 (*or enough to fit across front of Head*), sl st 2nd ch from hook, sl st in each of next 29 ch. (30 sl st)

Fasten off, leaving a long tail for sewing.

1. Position Headband across front of Head, over Rows 5-6 of Hair Bangs. Use long tail and yarn needle to secure each end of Headband to Hair Bangs at Hairline.

Three-Leaf Clover

Round 1: With Color C and smaller hook, make a magic ring, [ch 6, sl st in ring] 3 times; ch 6, sl st in 2nd ch from hook, sl st in each of next 4 ch, sl st in ring. (3 ch-6 loops & 5 sl st stem) *(image 15)*

Round 2: [(Sc, hdc, dc, htr, dc, hdc, dc, htr, dc, hdc, sc) in next ch-6 loop; sl st in magic ring] 3 times. *(image 16)* (3 Leaves)

Fasten off, leaving a long tail for sewing.

1. Position three-leaf clover to one side on Headband, and secure to Hair Bangs. *(image 17)*

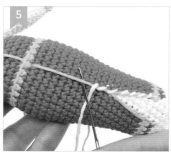

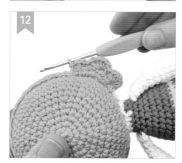

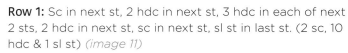

Martina

ARGENTINA

MARTINA in her traditional paisana ("country woman") dress and hat.

MATERIALS & TOOLS

YARN: HELLO Cotton

- **Main Color (MC):** Dark Beige (158) for Face & Arms
- **Color A:** Russet (168) for Hair
- **Color B:** Grey Blue (149) for Dress (trim)
- **Color C:** Cream (156) for Dress (main color)
- **Color D:** Black (160) for Hat
- Small amount of: Salmon (109) for Cheeks

HOOK SIZE: 2.5 mm hook
2.0 mm hook for Bib

OTHER: DMC Embroidery Floss - Black for Eyes and Mouth
Embroidery Needle
Stitch Marker
Yarn Needle
Stuffing
Straight Pins

HEAD

Follow instructions for Basic Doll Head - Front & Back.

Head Assembly

Follow Steps 1-7 of Basic Doll Head Assembly, and in Step 3, single crochet in each of next 45 stitches to complete the Hairline. (46 stitches)

ARM (Make 2)

Rounds 1-3: Follow instructions for Basic Doll Arm Rounds 1-3.

Change to Color B.

Round 4: Sc in each st around. (8 sc)

Round 5a: Working in front loops only, [sl st in next st, ch 2] 8 times, sl st in back loop of first sl st. (8 ch-2 loops)

Change to Color C (with a ch 1).

Round 5b: Working in unused back loops of Round 4, sc in each st around. (8 sc) (image 1)

Rounds 6-15: (10 rounds) Sc in each st around. (8 sc)

Fasten off.

1. Stuff the lower half of each Arm, leaving the remainder of Arm unstuffed.

2. Set Arms aside.

BODY

Rounds 1-13: Follow instructions for Basic Doll Body Base & Dress Rounds 1-13.

Change to Color C.

Round 14: Working in back loops only, sc in each st around. (26 sc)

Change to Color B.

Round 15: Working in back loops only, sc in each st around. (26 sc)

Change to Color C.

Round 16: Sc in each st around. (26 sc)

Rounds 17-30 (14 rounds): Follow instructions for Basic Doll Body Rounds 17-30.

Change to Color B.

Round 31: Sc in each st around. (35 sc)

Change to Color C.

Round 32: Working in back loops only, [sc in each each of next 3 sts, dec] 7 times. (28 sc)

Rounds 33-40: (8 rounds) Follow instructions for Basic Doll Body Rounds 33-40.

Change to MC.

Round 41: (Neck) Working in back loops only, sc in each st around. (16 sc)

Fasten off, leaving a long tail for sewing.

Base Trim: Follow instructions for Basic Doll Body Base Trim.

FINISHING DRESS - use photos as guide

Base Ruffle

Holding Dress upside down, attach Color B at back of Dress in first unworked front loop on Round 13. *(image 2)*

Round 1: Working in front loops only, sc in each st around. (26 sc)

Round 2: Sc in each of next 10 sts, inc in next st, sc in each of next 14 sts, inc in next st. (28 sc)

Round 3: [Skip next st, 5 hdc in next st, skip next st, sl st in next st] 7 times. (7 shells) *(image 3)*

Fasten off and weave in ends.

Dress Detail

With Color B and yarn needle, embroider designs (as shown) on Rounds 18, 21, 24 & 27, using short straight stitches. *(image 4)*

Waist Ruffle

Holding Dress upside down, attach Color B at back of Dress in first unworked front loop on Round 31. *(image 5)*

Round 1: Working in front loops only, 4 hdc in next st, skip next st, [sl st in next st, skip next st, 4 hdc in next st, skip next st] 8 times, sl st in same st as joining. (9 shells) *(image 6)*

Fasten off and weave in ends.

Bib & Buttons

Note: Bib is worked in rows, across both sides of the starting chain.

Row 1: *(Right Side)* With Color C and smaller hook, ch 5, sc in 2nd ch from hook, sc in next 2 ch, 3 sc in last ch; working on other side of starting ch, sc in each of next 3 ch. (9 sc)

Row 2: Ch 1, turn, sc in first st, sc in each of next 2 sts, inc in next st, sc in next st, inc in next st, sc in each of next 3 sts. (11 sc)

Change to Color B (Cut Color C, leaving a long tail for sewing).

Row 3: Ch 2, sl st in first st, [ch 2, sl st in next st] 10 times. (11 ch-2 loops & 11 sl sts)

Fasten off and weave in end.

1. Buttons - Split a length of Color B and embroider 3 French Knots down center of Bib. *(image 7)*

2. Using long tail of Color C and yarn needle, sew Row 2 of Bib to front of Dress, between Rounds 35-40, leaving Row 3 of Bib loose. *(image 8)*

DOLL ASSEMBLY

Follow Basic Doll Assembly Instructions.

HAIR

Hair Bangs

Note: The Hair Bangs are worked as a single piece in rows, starting with a magic ring.

Row 1: *(Wrong Side)* With Color A, make a magic ring, ch 3 *(counts as first dc, now and throughout)*, 5 dc in ring. (6 dc) Tighten ring but do not join round.

Row 2: *(Right Side)* Ch 3, turn, dc in first st, 2 dc in each of next 4 sts, 2 dc in last st *(3rd ch of ch-3)*. (12 dc)

Row 3: Ch 3, turn, dc in first st, [dc in next st, 2 dc in next st] 5 times, dc in last st. (18 dc)

Row 4: Ch 3, turn, 2 dc in next st, [dc in each of next 2 sts, 2 dc in next st] 5 times, dc in last st. (24 dc)

Row 5: Ch 3, turn, dc in each of next 9 sts, dc-dec. (11 dc) Leave remaining 12 sts unworked.

Row 6: Ch 2 *(counts as first hdc, now and throughout)*, turn, dc-dec *(using next 2 sts)*, htr in each of next 7 sts, htr in last st. *(3rd ch of ch-3)*. (1 hdc, 1 dc & 8 htr)

Row 7: Ch 3, turn, dc in each of next 3 sts, hdc in each of next 3 sts, sc in next st, dec *(using next st & 2nd ch of ch-2)*. (4 dc, 3 hdc & 2 sc)

Row 8: Ch 1, turn, skip first st, sc in next st, hdc in next st, dc in each of next 3 sts, htr in next st, dc in next st, dc in last st *(3rd ch of ch-3)*. (1 sc, 1 hdc, 5 dc & 1 htr)

Fasten off and weave in ends.

Row 5a: With right side facing, attach Color A to first st on Row 4 *(3rd ch of ch-3)*, ch 3 *(image 9)*, dc in each of next 9 sts, dc-dec. (11 dc)

Rows 6a-8a: Repeat Rows 6-8 of Hair Bangs.

Fasten off, leaving a long tail for sewing. *(image 10)*

1. Position Hair Bangs on Head Front, aligned with the Hairline. Gently shape to fit full length of Hairline, pinning in place. *(image 11)*

2. Use long tail and yarn needle to sew Hair Bangs to Hairline. *(images 12 & 13)*

Braids

1. Cut 24 strands of Color A, 12" (30 cm) in length.

2. Pull four (4) strands together, half-way through each of last 3 stitches on either side of Hair Bangs. (12 strands used per side) *(image 14)*

3. Separate the strands into 3 sections (about 8 strands each), and braid to desired length. *(image 15)*

4. Secure end of each Braid with a short strand of Color B, and trim the ends.

HAT

Round 1: With Color D, make a magic ring, ch 2, 8 hdc in ring; join with sl st to first hdc. (8 hdc)

Round 2: Ch 2, 2 hdc in each st around; join with sl st to first hdc. (16 hdc)

Round 3: Ch 1, working under both the back loop & 3rd loop together, sc in each st around; join with sl st to first sc. (16 sc)

Rounds 4-5: *(2 rounds)* Ch 1, sc in each st around; join with sl st to first sc. (16 sc)

Round 6: Ch 2, working in back loops only, 2 hdc in first st, [2 hdc in next st, hdc in next st, 2 hdc in next st] 5 times; join with sl st to first hdc. (27 hdc)

Round 7: Ch 2, hdc in first st, hdc in next st, 2 hdc in next st, [hdc in each of next 2 sts, 2 hdc in next st] 8 times; join with sl st to first hdc. (36 hdc) *(image 16)*

Fasten off, leaving a long tail for sewing.

FINISHING DOLL - use photos as guide

1. Follow Basic Doll Face Instructions *(image 17)*

2. With Color A, embroider additional hair bangs across one side of forehead using a few long stitches.

3. Use long tail and yarn needle to sew Hat to one side of Head. *(image 18)*

Elif

TURKIYE

ELIF in her Ottoman Era fez hat, veil and robe.

MATERIALS & TOOLS

YARN: HELLO Cotton

Main Color (MC): Misty Rose (163) - for Face & Arms

Color A: Dark Brown (127) - for Hair

Color B: Burgundy (116) - for Dress (Contrast)

Color C: Cherry Red (113) - for Dress & Hat (Main)

Color D: Dark Yellow (120) - for Dress & Hat (Trim)

Color E: Baby Pink (101) - for Veil

Small amount of: Salmon (109) for Cheeks

HOOK SIZE: 2.5 mm hook

OTHER: DMC Embroidery Floss - Black for Eyes and Mouth

Embroidery Needle

Stitch Marker

Yarn Needle

Stuffing

Straight Pins

ELIF

HEAD

Follow instructions for Basic Doll Head - Front & Back.

Head Assembly

Follow Steps 1-7 of Basic Doll Head Assembly, and in Step 3, single crochet in each of next 43 stitches to complete the Hairline. (44 stitches)

ARM (Make 2)

Rounds 1-3: Follow instructions for Basic Doll Arm Rounds 1-3. Change to Color C

Round 4: [Sc in next st, inc in next st] 4 times. (12 sc)

Rounds 5-14: *(10 rounds)* Sc in each st around. (12 sc)

Round 15: [Sc in next st, dec] 4 times. (8 sc)

Fasten off.

1. Stuff the lower half of each Arm, leaving the remainder of Arm unstuffed.

2. Set Arms aside.

BODY (Robe)

Rounds 1-16: Follow instructions for Basic Doll Body Base & Dress Rounds 1-16.

Change to Color D.

Round 17: Sc in each of next 3 sts, inc in next st, sc in each of next 13 sts, inc in next st, sc in each of next 8 sts. (28 sc)

Change to Color C.

Round 18: Working in back loops only, sc in each st around. (28 sc)

Continue in Color C.

Rounds 19-32: *(14 rounds)* Follow instructions for Basic Doll Body Dress Rounds 19-32.

Change to Color D.

Round 33: Sc in each st around. (28 sc)

Change to Color C.

Round 34: Working in back loops only, sc in each st around. (28 sc)

Notes for Color Changes from Round 35 onwards:

a. *Change color in the last step of the previous stitch.*

b. *Drop the non-working yarn to the wrong side, picking it up again for the next color change (stranding the yarn). Alternatively, cut and tie yarn ends on inside of Dress.*

Round 35: Sc in each of next 15 sc; with Color B, sc in next st; with Color C, sc in each of next 12 sts. (28 sc)

Round 36: Sc in each of next 8 sts, dec, sc in each of next 5 sts; with Color B, sc in each of next 2 sts; with Color C, sc in each of next 5 sts, dec, sc in each of next 4 sts. (26 sc)

Round 37: Sc in each of next 8 sts, dec, sc in each of next 4 sts; with Color B, sc in each of next 2 sts; with Color C, sc in each of next 5 sts, dec, sc in each of next 3 sts. (24 sc)

Round 38: [Sc in each of next 2 sts, dec] 3 times, sc in next st; with Color B, sc in each of next 3 sts; with Color C, dec, sc in each of next 2 sts, [dec] 2 times. (18 sc)

Note: *When attaching each Arm, flatten the top of the Arm and hold against the Body. Work the "attaching" stitches through both the layers of the Arm and the Body together.*

Round 39: *(Attaching Arms)* Sc in each of next 4 sts on Body; working on First Arm & Body, sc in each of next 4 sts *(First Arm attached)*; working on Body only, sc in each of next 2 sts; with Color B, sc in each of next 3 sts; with Color C, sc in next st; working on Second Arm & Body, sc in each of next 4 sts *(Second Arm attached)*. (18 sc)

Round 40: Sc in each of next 5 sts, dec, sc in each of next 3 sts; with Color B, sc in each of next 3 sts; with Color C, sc in each of next 2, dec, sc in next st. (16 sc)

Round 41: *(Neck)* Working in back loops only, sc in each of next 9 sts; working in both loops, sc in each of next 3 sts;

working in back loops only, sc in each of next 4 sts. (16 sc)

Fasten off, leaving a long tail for sewing. *(image 1)*

Base Trim: Follow instructions for Basic Doll Body Base Trim.

Belt Buckle:

Round 1: With Color D, make a magic ring; 6 sc in ring, sl st in first sc to join rnd. (6 sc)

Fasten off, leaving long tail for sewing.

ROBE DETAILS – use photos as guide

1. With Color D and yarn needle, embroider two long, straight stitches either side of Robe neckline, between Rounds 34 & 40 of Body, creating a "V" shape. *(image 2)*

2. Make another long straight stitch from base of "V" down front of Robe to Round 17. *(image 3)*

3. Use Fly Stitches to create decorative pattern on front of Robe, either side of long straight stitch, and on the outer side of the "V". *(images 4 & 5)*

TIP: *For ease of placement, follow natural alignment of crochet stitches to create a staggered effect.*

4. Position Belt Buckle at base of "V" and sew in place.

DOLL ASSEMBLY

Follow Basic Doll Assembly Instructions.

HAIR

Hair Piece (Make 2)

Row 1: With Color A, starting with long tail, ch 9; dc in 4th ch from hook *(skipped ch count as first dc)*, dc in each of next 3 ch, dc-dec *(using last 2 ch)*. (6 dc)

Row 2: Ch 2 *(counts as first st)*, turn, dc-dec *(using next 2 sts)*, htr in next st, tr in next st, tr in last st *(3rd ch of ch-3)*. (5 sts)

Fasten off, leaving a long tail for sewing. *(image 6)*

1. Position Hair Pieces on Head Front with starting chains across Rounds 9-13 and long finishing tails meeting end of Hairline.

2. Use long finishing tails and yarn needle to sew sides of Rows 1 & 2 of Hair Pieces to Hairline. *(image 7)*

3. Use starting tail and yarn needle to secure corner of Hair Pieces with one stitch to Face between Rounds 8 & 9. *(image 8)*

HAT ("Fez")

Round 1: With Color C, ch 21; sc in 2nd ch from hook, sc in each of next 18 ch, 3 sc in last ch; working on other side of starting ch, sc in each of next 8 ch, inc in last ch. (42 sc)

Round 2: Inc in next st, sc in each of next 19 sts, inc in next st, sc in each of next 21 sts. (44 sc) *(image 9)*

Round 3: Working under both the back loop & back bar together, [inc in next st, sc in each of next 21 sts] 2 times. (46 sc)

Round 4: Sc in each st around. (46 sc)

Round 5: Sc in next st, inc in next st, sc in each of next 22 sts, inc in next st, sc in each of next 21 sts. (48 sc)

Round 6: Sc in each st around. (48 sc) Sc in each of next 3 sts *(to move the end of round to side of Hat)*.

Work continues in Rows.

Row 1: *(Wrong Side)* Ch 1, turn, sc in first st, sc in each of next 25 sts. (26 sc) Leave remaining sts unworked.

Rows 2-3: *(2 rows)* Ch 1, turn, sc in each st across. (26 sc) *(image 10)*

Row 4: *(Right Side)* Ch 1, turn, sc in first st, sc in each of next 24 sts, inc in last st. (27 sc)

Row 5: Ch 1, turn, sc in first st, sc in each of next 25 sts, inc in last st. (28 sc)

Fasten off, leaving a long tail for sewing.

Small Coin (Make 4)

Round 1: With Color D, make a magic ring; 6 sc in ring, sl st in first sc to join round. (6 sc)

Fasten off, leaving long tail for sewing.

Large Coin (Make 1)

Round 1: With Color D, make a magic ring; ch 1, 8 hdc in ring, sl st in first hdc to join round. (8 hdc)

Fasten off, leaving long tail for sewing.

Finishing Hat - use photos as guide

1. Position Coins on front of Hat over Rows 1-5, with Large Coin positioned in the center, and using long tails and yarn needle, sew Coins in place.

2. With Color D, add a Fly Stitch above each Coin and then embroider a series of straight stitches between the Fly Stitches to connect the Coins. *(image 11)*

3. Position Hat on Head, with Row 5 aligned with the two Hair Pieces. *(image 12)*

4. Use long tail and yarn needle to sew last 4 rows of Hat to Hairline (taking care to keep shape of Hat). *(image 13)*

5. Lightly stuff top corners of Hat, then whipstitch to secure Hat across back of Head. *(image 14)*

6. On other side of Hat, sew last 4 rows to Hairline, leaving the front of the Hat unsewn.

VEIL

Note: *Adjust length of Veil to fit Head by adding or removing rows before fastening off.*

Row 1: With Color E, starting with long tail, ch 5, sc in 2nd ch from hook, sc in each of next 3 ch. (4 sc)

Rows 2-53: *(52 rows)* Ch 1, turn, sc in each st across. (4 sc)

Fasten off, leaving a long tail for sewing.

FINISHING DOLL - use photos as guide

1. Follow Basic Doll Face Instructions *(image 15)*

2. Position beginning and end of Veil in line with top corners of Hat, allowing Veil to drape around back of Head and Neck.

3. Use long tails and yarn needle, whipstitch ends of Veil to unworked front loops on Round 2 of Hat. *(image 16)*

4. Use a discrete stitch to secure Veil to back of Neck (optional). *(images 17 & 18)*

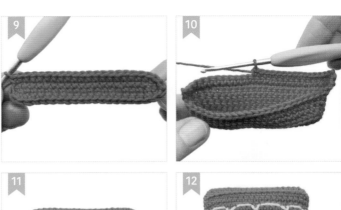

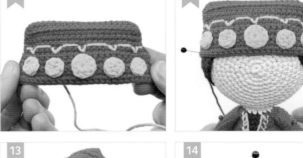

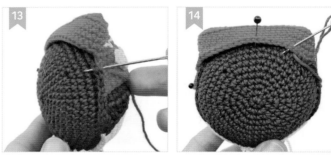

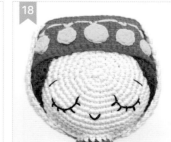

Greta

GERMANY

GRETA in her traditional dirndl dress.

MATERIALS & TOOLS

YARN: HELLO Cotton

- **Main Color (MC):** Misty Rose (163) for Face & Arms
- **Color A:** Ginger Root (165) for Hair
- **Color B:** Dark Green (135) for Dress
- **Color C:** Burgundy (116) for Dress
- **Color D:** Black (160) for Dress
- **Color E:** White (154) for Blouse & Apron
- Small amount of: Salmon (109) for Cheeks

HOOK SIZE: 2.5 mm hook

OTHER: DMC Embroidery Floss - Black for Eyes and Mouth

Embroidery Needle

Stitch Marker

Yarn Needle

Stuffing

Straight Pins

HEAD

Follow instructions for Basic Doll Head - Front & Back.

Head Assembly

Follow Steps 1-7 of Basic Doll Head Assembly, and in Step 3, single crochet in each of next 43 stitches to complete the Hairline. (44 stitches)

ARM (Make 2)

Rounds 1-9: Follow instructions for Basic Doll Arm Rounds 1-9.

Change to Color E.

Round 10: Sc in each st around. (8 sc)

Round 11a: Working in front loops only, [sl st in next st, ch 2] 8 times, sl st in back loop of first sl st. (8 ch-2 loops)

Round 11b: Working in unused back loops of Round 10, inc in each st around. (16 sc)

Rounds 12-13: *(2 rounds)* Sc in each st around. (16 sc)

Round 14: [Sc in next st, dec, sc in next st] 4 times. (12 sc)

Round 15: [Sc in next st, dec] 4 times. (8 sc)

Fasten off. *(image 1)*

1. Stuff the lower half of each Arm, leaving the remainder of Arm unstuffed.

2. Set Arms aside.

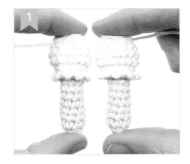

BODY

Notes for Color Changes from Round 37 onwards:

a. *Change color in the last step of the previous stitch.*

b. *Drop the non-working yarn to the wrong side, picking it up again for the next color change (stranding the yarn). Alternatively, cut and tie yarn ends on inside of Dress.*

Rounds 1-30: Follow instructions for Basic Doll Body Base & Dress Rounds 1-30.

Change to Color C.

Round 31: Working in back loops only, sc in each st around. (35 sc)

Round 32: [Sc in each each of next 3 sts, dec] 7 times. (28 sc)

Change to Color D.

135

Round 33: Working in back loops only, sc in each st around. (28 sc)

Rounds 34-35: *(2 rounds)* Sc in each st around. (28 sc)

Round 36: Sc in each of next 8 sts, dec, sc in each of next 12 sts, dec, sc in each of next 4 sts. (26 sc)

Round 37: With Color D, sc in each of next 8 sts, dec, sc in each of next 2 sts; with Color E, sc in back loops only of each of next 6 sts; with Color D, sc in each of next 3 sts, dec, sc in each of next 3 sts. (24 sc)

Round 38: With Color D, [dec, sc in each of next 2 sts] 2 times, dec, sc in next st; with MC, working in back loops only, sc in next st, dec, sc in each of next 3 sts; with Color D, dec, sc in each of next 2 sts, dec, sc in next st. (18 sc)

Note: *When attaching each Arm, flatten the top of the Arm and hold against the Body. Work the "attaching" stitches through both the layers of the Arm and the Body together.*

Round 39: *(Attaching Arms)* Sc in each of next 4 sts on Body; working on First Arm & Body, sc in each of next 4 sts *(First Arm attached)*; working on Body only, sc in next st; with MC, sc in each of next 4 sts; with Color D, sc in next st; working on Second Arm & Body, sc in each of next 4 sts *(Second Arm attached)*. (18 sc)

Round 40: With MC, sc in each of next 4 sts; working in back loops only, sc in next st, dec, sc in each of next 2 sts; working through both loops, sc in each of next 4 sts; working in back loops only, sc in each of next 2 sts, dec, sc in next st. (16 sc)

Round 41: *(Neck)* Sc in each st around. (16 sc)

Fasten off, leaving a long tail for sewing. *(image 2)*

Base Trim: Follow instructions for Basic Doll Body Base Trim.

APRON

Row 1: *(Right Side)* With Color E, starting with long tail, ch 6, sc in 2nd ch from hook, sc in each of next 4 ch. (5 sc)

Row 2: Ch 1, turn, sc in each st across. (5 sc)

Row 3: Ch 1, turn, inc in next st, sc in each of next 3 sts, inc in last st. (7 sc)

Rows 4-11: *(8 rows)* Ch 1, turn, sc in each st across. (7 sc)

Edging Round: Ch 1 (do not turn), working in sides of

rows, sc in each of next 10 rows; ch 1, working on other side of starting ch, sc in each of next 5 ch, ch 1; working in sides of rows, sc in each of next 10 rows; ch 1, sl st in first sc on Row 11.

Fasten off and weave in end.

DRESS DETAILS - use photos as guide

1. Split a length of Color E and embroider 3 "X"s (using straight stitches) on Dress Front over Rounds 34 to 36. *(image 3)*

2. With Color D, make a few small vertical straight stitches at the Neckline of the Dress, to neaten color changes. (Optional)

3. Split lengths of Color B and Color C to embroider a decorative border along bottom of Apron (Rows 9 & 10). *(image 4)*

4. Use starting tail of Apron to sew it to unworked front loops on Round 32 of Body, centered at the front.

HAIR

Hair Bangs

Note: *The Hair Bangs are worked as a single piece in rows, starting with a magic ring.*

Row 1: *(Wrong Side)* With Color A, make a magic ring, ch 3 *(counts as first dc, now and throughout)*, 5 dc in ring. (6 dc) Tighten ring but do not join round.

Row 2: *(Right Side)* Ch 3, turn, dc in first st, 2 dc in each of next 4 sts, 2 dc in last st *(3rd ch of ch-3)*. (12 dc)

Row 3: Ch 3, turn, dc in first st, [dc in next st, 2 dc in next st] 5 times, dc in last st. (18 dc)

Row 4: Ch 3, turn, 2 dc in next st, [dc in each of next 2 sts, 2 dc in next st] 5 times, dc in last st. (24 dc)

Row 5: Ch 3, turn, htr in each of next 4 sts, dc in next st, dc-dec *(using next 2 sts)*. (3 dc & 4 htr) Leave remaining 16 sts unworked.

Row 6: Ch 2 *(counts as first hdc, now and throughout)*, turn, dc-dec *(using next 2 sts)*, htr in each of next 3 sts, htr in last st. *(3rd ch of ch-3)* (1 hdc, 1 dc & 4 htr)

Row 7: Ch 3, turn, dc in next st, hdc in next st, sc in next st, dec *(using next st & 2nd ch of ch-2)*. (2 dc, 1 hdc & 2 sc)

Row 8: Ch 1, turn, skip first st, sc in next st, hdc in next st, dc in next st, htr in last st *(3rd ch of ch-3)*. (1 sc, 1 hdc, 1 dc & 1 htr)

Fasten off and weave in ends.

Row 5a: With right side facing, attach Color A to first st on Row 4 *(3rd ch of ch-3)*, ch 3 *(image 5)*, htr in each of next 4 sts, dc in next st, dc-dec *(using next 2 sts)*. (3 dc & 4 htr) Leave remaining 8 sts unworked.

Rows 6a-8a: Repeat Rows 6-8 of Hair Bangs.

Fasten off, leaving a long tail for sewing. *(image 6)*

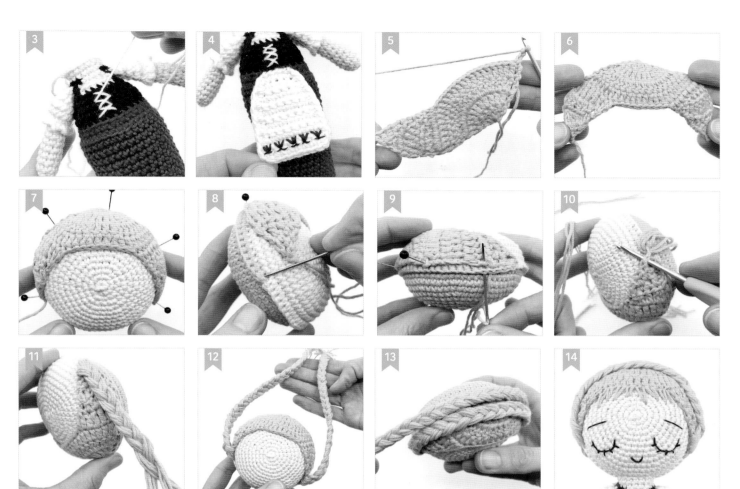

1. Position Hair Bangs on Head Front, aligned with the Hairline. Gently shape to fit full length of Hairline, pinning in place. *(image 7)*

2. Use long tail and yarn needle to sew Hair Bangs to Hairline. *(images 8 & 9)*

Braids

1. Cut 18 strands of Color A, about 20" (50 cm) in length.

2. Holding Head upside down, pull three (3) strands together, half-way through each of last 3 stitches on either side of Hair Bangs. (9 strands used per side) *(image 10)*

3. Separate the strands into 3 sections (about 6 strands each), and braid to desired length. *(image 11)*

4. Secure end of each Braid with a short strand of yarn, and trim the ends. *(image 12)*

5. Wrap Braids over top of Head *(image 13)* and use a discrete stitch to secure ends at back of Head.

DOLL ASSEMBLY

Follow Basic Doll Assembly Instructions.

FINISHING DOLL - use photos as guide

1. Follow Basic Doll Face Instructions.

2. With Color A, embroider additional hair bangs across forehead using straight stitches. *(image 14)*

Zinira

UZBEKISTAN

ZINIRA in her traditional khan atlas robe and doppa hat.

Uzbekistan is famous for its beautiful, handwoven silk "ikat" fabrics, called "khan-atlas".

MATERIALS & TOOLS

YARN: HELLO Cotton

- **Main Color (MC):** Ivory (173) for Face & Arms
- **Color A:** Dark Brown (127) for Hair
- **Color B:** Sea Green (136) for Robe
- **Color C:** Golden Yellow (121) for Robe & Hat detail
- **Color D:** Purple (143) for Robe detail & Hat
- **Color E:** Cherry Red (113) for Robe detail
- **Color F:** White (154) for Robe detail
- **Color G:** Black (160) for Vest
- Small amount of: Salmon (109) for Cheeks

HOOK SIZE: 2.5 mm hook

OTHER: DMC Embroidery Floss - Black for Eyes and Mouth
Embroidery Needle
Stitch Marker
Yarn Needle
Stuffing
Straight Pins

ZINIRA

HEAD

Follow instructions for Basic Doll Head - Front & Back.

Head Assembly

Follow Steps 1-7 of Basic Doll Head Assembly, and in Step 3, single crochet in each of next 43 stitches to complete the Hairline. (44 stitches)

ARM (Make 2)

Rounds 1-3: Follow instructions for Basic Doll Arm Rounds 1-3.

Change to Color B.

Round 4-15: *(12 rounds)* Sc in each st around. (8 sc)

Fasten off.

1. Stuff the lower half of each Arm, leaving the remainder of Arm unstuffed.

2. Set Arms aside.

BODY (Robe)

Rounds 1-40: Follow instructions for Basic Doll Body Base & Dress Rounds 1-40.

Change to MC.

Round 41: *(Neck)* Sc in each st around. (16 sc)

Fasten off, leaving a long tail for sewing.

Base Trim: Follow instructions for Basic Doll Body Base Trim.

ROBE DETAILS - use photos as guide

Note: *Details are embroidered using a yarn needle. For ease of stitch placement, embroider between crochet stitches.*

1. With Color C, embroider 3 sets of large "zig-zags" over Rounds 13-16, Rounds 21-24 & Rounds 29-32, using long straight stitches - 4 rounds tall and 4 stitches wide. *(image 1)*

2. With Color D:

a) Backstitch around the base of each set of zig-zags. *(image 2)*

b) Embroider small triangles inside the zig-zag triangles - 2 rounds tall and 2 stitches wide.

c) Embroider taller triangles below the top two backstitch lines - 3 rounds tall and 2 stitches wide - in line with the small triangles. *(image 3)*

3. With Color E:

a) Embroider 3 rounds of small zig-zags over Rounds 17, 25 & 33 - 1 round tall and 1 stitch wide. *(image 4)*

b) Add small zig-zag stitches inside the large zig zags of Color C. *(image 5)*

4. With Color F:

a) Under backstitches (Round 12), embroider a round of small zig-zags - 1 round tall and 1 stitch wide.

b) On Round 4 of each Sleeve, embroider small zig-zags around. *(image 6)*

c) Embroider upside-down "V"s between the large triangles - 3 rounds tall and 2 stitches wide - over Rounds 18-20 & Rounds 26-28. *(image 7)*

VEST

Note: *Vest is worked from top down.*

Row 1: *(Wrong Side)* With Color G, ch 23, sc in 2nd ch from from hook, sc in each of next 21 ch. (22 sc)

Row 2: *(Right Side)* Ch 1, turn, sc in first st, sc in next st, ch 4, skip next 4 sts *(First Armhole)*, sc in each of next 10 sts, ch 4, skip next 4 sts *(Second Armhole)*, sc in each of next 2 sts. (14 sc & 2 ch-4 loops)

Row 3: Ch 1, turn, inc in first st, sc in next st; working in ch-4, sc in each of next 4 ch; sc in each of next 10 sts; working in ch-4, sc in each of next 4 ch; sc in next st, inc in last st. (24 sc)

Row 4: Ch 1, turn, sc in first st, sc in each of next 2 sts, [inc in next st, sc in each of next 3 sts] 5 times, sc in last st. (29 sc)

Row 5: Ch 1, turn, inc in first st, [sc in each of next 13 sts, inc in next st] 2 times. (32 sc)

Row 6: Ch 1, turn, sc in each st across. (32 sc)

Fasten off and weave in ends. *(image 8)*

1. With Color C and yarn needle, with right side facing, embroider small backstitches across fronts and bottom of Vest. *(image 9)*.

DOLL ASSEMBLY

Follow Basic Doll Assembly Instructions.

HAIR

Hair Piece (Make 2)

Row 1: With Color A, starting with long tail, ch 9; dc in 4th ch from hook *(skipped ch count as first dc)*, dc in each of next 3 ch, dc-dec *(using last 2 ch)*. (6 dc)

Row 2: Ch 2 *(counts as first st)*, turn, dc-dec *(using next 2 sts)*, htr in next st, tr in next st, tr in last st *(3rd ch of ch-3)*. (5 sts)

Fasten off, leaving a long tail for sewing. *(image 10)*

1. Position Hair Pieces on Head Front with starting chains across Rounds 9-13 and long finishing tails meeting end of Hairline. *(image 11)*

2. Use long finishing tails and yarn needle to sew sides of Rows 1 & 2 of Hair Pieces to Hairline. *(image 12)*

3. Use starting tail and yarn needle to secure corner of Hair Pieces with one stitch to Face between Rounds 8 & 9. *(image 13)*

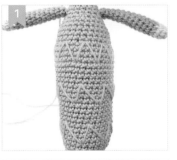

Braids

1. Cut 12 strands of Color A, 10" (25 cm) in length.

2. Assemble into four (4) bundles of three (3) strands each - two bundles per side.

3. Use crochet hook to pull first bundle half-way through the last stitch on Hairline.

4. Divide the "half-length" strands into three (3) sections and braid together, securing with short strand of Color A.

5. On same side of Head, pull next bundle half-way through the next stitch on Hairline *(image 14)* and repeat step 4. *(images 15 & 16)*

6. Repeat steps 3-5 on other side of Head.

7. Trim the ends.

FINISHING FACE - use photos as guide

1. Follow Basic Doll Face Instructions.

2. With Color A, embroider additional hair bangs across one side of forehead using a few long stitches.

HAT ("Doppa")

Round 1: With Color D, ch 21; sc in 2nd ch from hook, sc in each of next 18 ch, 3 sc in last ch; working on other side of starting ch, sc in each of next 8 ch, inc in last ch. (42 sc)

Round 2: Inc in next st, sc in each of next 19 sts, inc in next st, sc in each of next 21 sts. (44 sc) *(image 17)*

Round 3: Working under both the back loop & back bar loop together, [inc in next st, sc in each of next 21 sts] 2 times. (46 sc)

Round 4: Sc in each st around. (46 sc)

Round 5: Sc in next st, inc in next st, sc in each of next 22 sts, inc in next st, sc in each of next 21 sts. (48 sc)

Round 6: Sc in each st around. (48 sc) Sc in each of next 3 sts *(to move the end of round to side of Hat).*

Work continues in Rows.

Row 1: *(Wrong Side)* Ch 1, turn, sc in first st, sc in each of next 25 sts. (26 sc) Leave remaining sts unworked.

Rows 2-3: *(2 rows)* Ch 1, turn, sc in each st across. (26 sc) *(image 18)*

Row 4: *(Right Side)* Ch 1, turn, sc in first st, sc in each of next 24 sts, inc in last st. (27 sc)

Row 5: Ch 1, turn, sc in first st, sc in each of next 25 sts, inc in last st. (28 sc)

Fasten off, leaving a long tail for sewing.

1. With Color C and yarn needle, embroider zig-zags over Rows 1 & 2.

2. Embroider French Knots around Hat between Rows 4 & 5. *(image 19)*

FINISHING DOLL - use photos as guide

1. Place Vest on Doll.

2. Position Hat on Head, with Row 5 aligned with the two Hair Pieces.

3. Use long tail and yarn needle to sew last 4 rows of Hat to Hairline (taking care to keep shape of Hat). *(image 20)*

4. Lightly stuff top corners of Hat, then whipstitch to secure Hat across back of Head. *(image 21)*

5. On other side of Hat, sew last 4 rows to Hairline, leaving the front of the Hat unsewn. *(image 22)*

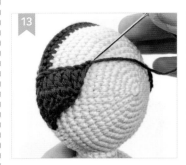

Liliana

SPAIN

LILIANA in her traditional traje de flamenca (flamenco outfit).

MATERIALS & TOOLS

YARN: HELLO Cotton

- **Main Color (MC):** Misty Rose (163) for Face & Arms
- **Color A:** Dark Brown (127) for Hair
- **Color B:** Red (114) for Dress (main)
- **Color C:** Black (160) for Dress (trim)
- Small amount of: Salmon (109) for Cheeks

HOOK SIZE: 2.5 mm hook

OTHER: DMC Embroidery Floss - Black for Eyes and Mouth

Embroidery Needle

Stitch Marker

Yarn Needle

Stuffing

Straight Pins

HEAD

Follow instructions for Basic Doll Head - Front & Back.

Head Assembly

Follow Steps 1-7 of Basic Doll Head Assembly, and in Step 3, single crochet in each of next 43 stitches to complete the Hairline. (44 stitches)

ARM (Make 2)

Rounds 1-6: Follow instructions for Basic Doll Arm Rounds 1-6.

Change to Color B.

Rounds 7-15: *(9 rounds)* Sc in each st around. (8 sc)

Fasten off.

1. Stuff the lower half of each Arm, leaving the remainder of Arm unstuffed.

2. Set Arms aside.

BODY

Note: *In Rounds 12-26, the* underlined italics *instructions indicate these stitches to be worked in back loops only. All other stitches worked in both loops. The unworked front loops of these stitches will be used for making the Skirt Ruffles. It may be helpful to use a running stitch marker for these rounds.*

Rounds 1-11: Follow instructions for Basic Doll Body Base & Dress Rounds 1-11.

Round 12: Sc in each of next 5 sts; working in back loops only, *inc in next st, sc in each of next 12 sts, inc in next st, sc in each of next 3 sts*; working in both loops, sc in each of next 2 sts. (26 sc)

Round 13: Sc in each each of next 5 sts, *sc in next st*, sc in each of next 18 sts, *sc in next st,* sc in next st. (26 sc)

Round 14: Sc in each of next 5 sts, *sc in next st,* sc in each of next 4 sts, *sc in each of next 12 sts*, sc in each of next 3 sts, *sc in next st.* (26 sc)

Round 15: Sc in each of next 5 sts, *sc in next st*, sc in each of next 3 sts, *sc in next st*, sc in each of next 13 sts, *sc in next st*, sc in each of next 2 sts. (26 sc)

Round 16: *Sc in next st*, sc in each each of next 4 sts, *sc in next st*, sc in each of next 2 sts, *sc in next st*, sc in each of next 3 sts, *sc in each of next 10 sts*, sc in each of next 2 sts, *sc in next st*, sc in next st. (26 sc)

Round 17: Sc in next st, *sc in next st*, sc in each of next 3 sts, *sc in next st*, inc in next st, *sc in next st*, sc in each of next 3 sts, *sc in next st*, sc in each of next 8 sts, inc in next st, sc in each of next 4 sts, *sc in next st*. (28 sc)

Round 18: [Sc in each of next 2 sts, *sc in next st*] 4 times, sc in each of next 13 sts, *sc in next st*, sc in each of next 2 sts. (28 sc)

Round 19: *Sc in next st*, sc in each of next 2 sts, *sc in each of next 3 sts*, [sc in each of next 2 sts, *sc in next st*] 2 times, sc in each of next 14 sts, *sc in next st*, sc in next st. (28 sc)

Round 20: Sc in next st, *sc in next st*, sc in each of next 6 sts, *sc in next st,* sc in each of next 2 sts, *sc in next st*, sc in each of next 15 sts, *sc in next st*. (28 sc)

Round 21: Sc in each of next 2 sts, *sc in next st*, sc in each of next 5 sts, *sc in next st*, sc in each of next 2 sts, *sc in next st*, sc in each of next 16 sts. (28 sc)

Round 22: *Sc in next st*, sc in each each of next 2 sts, *sc in next st*, sc in each of next 3 sts, *inc in next st*, sc in each of next 3 sts, *sc in next st*, sc in each of next 10 sts, inc in next st, sc in each of next 5 sts. (30 sc)

Round 23: Sc in next st, *sc in next st*, sc in each of next 2 sts, *sc in each of next 4 sts*, sc in each of next 3 sts, *sc in next st*, sc in each of next 18 sts. (30 sc)

Round 24: Sc in each of next 2 sts, *sc in next st*, sc in each of next 7 sts, *sc in next st*, sc in each of next 19 sts. (30 sc)

Round 25: Sc in each of next 3 sts, *sc in next st*, sc in each of next 5 sts, *sc in next st*, sc in each of next 20 sts. (30 sc)

Round 26: Sc in each of next 4 sts, *sc in each of next 5 sts*, sc in each of next 21 sts. (30 sc)

Rounds 27-38: Follow instructions for Basic Doll Body Dress Rounds 27-38.

Note: *When attaching each Arm, flatten the top of the Arm and hold against the Body. Work the "attaching" stitches through both the layers of the Arm and the Body together.*

Change to MC.

Round 39: *(Attaching Arms)* Sc in each of next 4 sts on Body; working on First Arm & Body, sc in each of next 4 sts *(First Arm attached)*; working on Body only, sc in next st, working in back loops only, sc in each of next 4 sts, working in both loops, sc in next st; working on Second Arm & Body, sc in each of next 4 sts *(Second Arm attached)*. (18 sc)

Round 40: Sc in each of next 5 sts, dec, sc in each of next 8 sts, dec, sc in next st. (16 sc)

Round 41: *(Neck)* Sc in each st around. (16 sc)

Fasten off, leaving a long tail for sewing. *(image 1)*

Base Trim: Follow instructions for Basic Doll Body Base Trim.

DRESS DETAILS- use photos as guide

Note: *The Ruffles and Neckline Trim are worked holding the Doll upside down.*

Base Ruffle

Round 1: Attach Color B at back of Dress to 2nd unworked front loop on Round 11 *(image 2)*, ch 2, working in front loops

only, 2 dc in same st as joining, 2 dc in each of next 15 sts; following diagonal line of front loops to Round 17, 2 dc in each st *(image 3)*; working in Round 18, 2 dc in each of next 3 sts; following the diagonal to Round 12, 2 dc in each st; 2 dc in skipped first st on Round 11; join with sl st to first dc. (62 dc)

Change to Color C *(before joining at end of Round 1)*.

Round 2: Ch 1, inc in each st around; join with sl st to first sc. (124 sc) *(image 4)*

Fasten off and weave in ends.

Middle Ruffle

Round 1: Attach Color B at back of Dress to 2nd unworked front loop on Round 13 *(image 5)*, ch 2, working in front loops only, 2 dc in same st as joining, 2 dc in each of next 10 sts *(image 6)*; following diagonal line of front loops to Round 21, 2 dc in each st; working in Round 22, 2 dc in each of next 4 sts; following the diagonal to Round 14, 2 dc in each st; 2 dc in skipped first st on Round 13; join with sl st to first dc. (62 dc)

Change to Color C *(before joining at end of Round 1)*.

Round 2: Ch 1, inc in each st around; join with sl st to first sc. (124 sc)

Fasten off and weave in ends.

Top Ruffle

Round 1: Attach Color B at back of Dress to 2nd unworked front loop on Round 15 *(image 7)*, ch 2, working in front loops only, 2 dc in same st as joining, 2 dc in each of next 8 sts; following diagonal line of front loops to Round 24, 2 dc in each st; working in Round 25, 2 dc in each of next 5 sts; following the diagonal to Round 16, 2 dc in each st; 2 dc in skipped first st on Round 15; join with sl st to first dc. (64 dc)

Change to Color C *(before joining at end of Round 1)*.

Round 2: Ch 1, inc in each st around; join with sl st to first sc. (128 sc)

Fasten off and weave in ends.

Neckline Trim

Row 1: Working in unworked front loops on Round 38, attach Color C to first st *(image 8)*, sc in first front loop, ch 2, [sc in next st, ch 2] 2 times, sl st in last st.

Fasten off and weave in ends. *(image 9)*

DOLL ASSEMBLY

Follow Basic Doll Assembly Instructions.

HAIR

Hair Bangs & Side Bun

Note: *The Hair Bangs are worked as a single piece in rows, starting with a magic ring.*

Row 1: *(Wrong Side)* With Color A, make a magic ring, ch 3 *(counts as first dc, now and throughout)*, 5 dc in ring. (6 dc) Tighten ring but do not join round.

Row 2: *(Right Side)* Ch 3, turn, dc in first st, 2 dc in each of next 4 sts, 2 dc in last st *(3rd ch of ch-3)*. (12 dc)

Row 3: Ch 3, turn, dc in first st, [dc in next st, 2 dc in next st] 5 times, dc in last st. (18 dc)

Row 4: Ch 3, turn, 2 dc in next st, [dc in each of next 2 sts, 2 dc in next st] 5 times, dc in last st. (24 dc)

Row 5: Ch 3, turn, dc in each of next 22 sts, dc in last st. (24 dc)

Row 6: Turn, skip first 2 sts, 6 hdc in next st, skip next st, sl st in each of next 2 sts, skip next st, 6 hdc in next st, skip next st, sl st in each of next 2 sts, skip next 2 sts, 7 dc in next st, skip next 2 sts, sl st in each of next 2 sts, skip

next 2 sts, 4 tr in next st, tr in each of next 2 sts, tr in last st. (2 hdc-6 shells, 1 dc-7 shell, 7 tr & 6 sl sts) *(image 10)*

Side Bun: Ch 6, place stitch marker in last *(6th)* ch *(image 11)*, ch 30; 2 hdc in 3rd ch from hook, 2 hdc in each of next 27 ch *(to reach marker) (image 12)*, sc in each of next 6 ch, sl st in 2nd last tr on Row 6 to secure. *(image 13)*

Fasten off, leaving a long tail for sewing.

1. Coil the hdc-stitches in a tight, circular hair bun and secure with a few stitches. *(image 14)*

2. Position Hair Bangs and Side Bun on front of Head and gently shape to fit full length of hairline (allowing space for Side Bun), securing with straight pins. *(image 15)*

3. Use long tail and yarn needle to sew Hair Bangs to Hairline. *(image 16)*

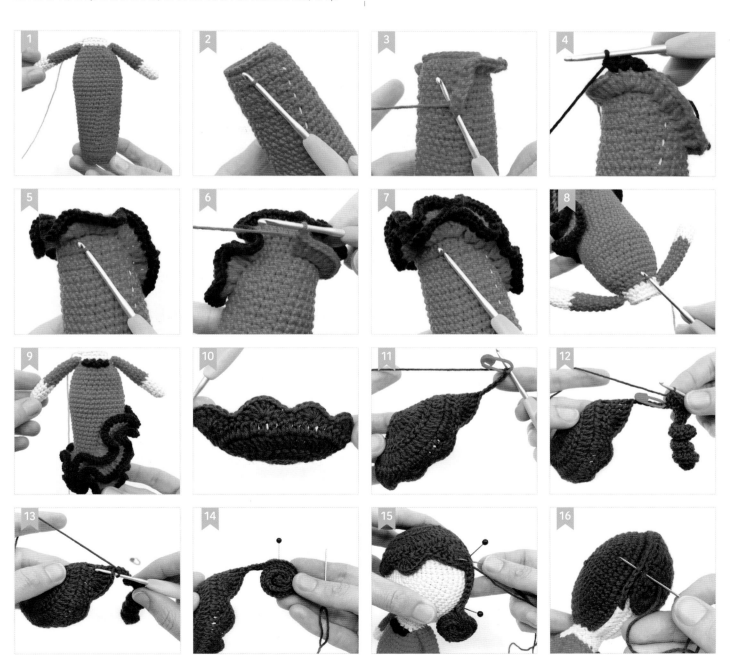

Flower

Round 1: With Color B, make a magic ring, 6 sc in ring. (6 sc)

Round 2: Working in front loops only, [(hdc, sc) in next st, hdc in next st] 3 times. (9 sts)

Round 3: Working in unworked back loops from Round 1, [(dc, hdc) in next st] 6 times. (12 sts)

Fasten off, leaving a long tail for sewing.

Forehead Curl

Row 1: *(Right Side)* With Color A, ch 15, sl st in 2nd ch from hook, inc in next ch, [sc in next ch, inc in next ch] 2 times,

sl st in each of next 8 ch. (8 sc & 9 sl sts)

Fasten off, leaving a long tail for sewing.

FINISHING DOLL - use photos as guide

1. Follow Basic Doll Face Instructions.

2. With Color B, embroider small Lips in center of Mouth.

3. Use yarn needle to secure Flower to side of Head, just above Side Bun. *(image 17)*

4. With wrong side facing, *(image 18)* position Forehead Curl to front of Head, between Hair Bangs and Side Bun, and using long tail and yarn needle, sew in place. *(image 19)*